BUT YOU CAN'T LEAVE, SHIRLEY

Barbara Land
my best regards,

Shirley A. Porter

Sept. 7, 1995

Goldfield Hotel, Goldfield Nevada.

BUT YOU CAN'T LEAVE, SHIRLEY

SHIRLEY A. PORTER

WESTERN BOOK / JOURNAL PRESS
SAN MATEO, CALIFORNIA

1992

ISBN: 0-936029-28-5
Library of Congress Catalog Number: 92-64097

Copyright 1992 by Shirley Porter Dybicz
All Rights Reserved
Manufactured in the United States of America

Western Book / Journal Press
Printers & Publishers
San Mateo, California 94402
1992

Library of Congress Cataloging-in-Publication Data
    Porter, Shirley
        But You Can't Leave, Shirley
        Goldfield Hotel
        Goldfield, Nevada

Photographs: Courtesy of the Nevada Historical Society

DEDICATION
DENNIS W. DYBICZ

To Dennis who is as much a part of this book as I am. It is not my account of the past fifteen years, it is ours.

For it was Dennis who was always with me sharing the hopes and dreams, the struggles and trials and the eventual loss of our beautiful Goldfield Hotel.

Dennis W. Dybicz

AUTHOR'S NOTE

At the time I purchased the Goldfield Hotel in 1976 I enjoyed what is called an average lifestyle. I was maintaining a home for my two youngest children and managing our own business.

There was nothing extraordinary about my life or the manner in which I lived it and the most important and rewarding role in my life was that of being a mother.

Therefore I was totally unprepared for and completely shocked by the encounters in the old building. I never expected nor wanted these strange events to occur. I have written these events exactly as they occurred but in no way does this story reflect all of the unusual incidents that I experienced in the hotel on a daily basis.

It is difficult for me to accept what took place in the hotel and I realize that others will find it equally difficult but this is a true and actual account of what happened.

Goldfield, Nevada

Nestled in the shadows of the Columbia and Malapia mountains on U.S. Highway 95 between Reno and Las Vegas lies Goldfield which, by 1907, was the largest city in Nevada. Goldfield came into being shortly after the discovery of gold by two prospectors named Harry Stimler and Billy Marsh during a severe sandstorm in December of 1902 in what was then called the Grandpa district. It was this discovery that led to the opening of the first mine aptly named the "Sandstorm".

The first town to be developed near this site was called Columbia and later the surrounding district became known as Goldfield, so named because it was a *"Virtual field of gold"*.

Goldfield Hotel at Crook (now Highway 95) and Columbia

By 1904 Goldfield was booming and changing from a huge tent city to a metropolis housing many fine restaurants, banks, hotels and residences. It catered to financiers from all over the world including the noted Bernard Baruch of New York as gold was being produced by the millions.

By 1907 Goldfield became the county seat of Esmeralda County, was second only to San Francisco in postal revenues for the western states, and its menus were comparable to the best dining houses in the nation. Main streets were inundated by saloons, banks, mercantile and hardware stores, bakeries and groceries where boistrous miners and elegant ladies walked the same paths. Electric lights were strung across the streets to illuminate this city where activity abounded twenty-four hours a day. Goldfield had its own brewery to service its numerous saloons, several newspapers to supply its residents with current events both local and nationwide, its own stock exchange, telephone and telegraph offices, men and women's organizations and, not to be excluded, fifty-three bordellos in its infamous red light district. Churches, hospitals, theaters and assay offices also sprang up rapidly among the hubbub of this teeming gold rush community where parades and social activities were in abundance and where one could become a millionaire overnight.

With the surge of businesses and population plus the lure of the gold mines, this newly established city not only attracted the heads of finance, politicians, famous entertainers and the elite of society, it also drew con men perpetrating their scams, highgrading miners and a few known gunmen into the area.

Goldfield was elegance from its strolling violinists at the Palm Grill to its high fashion and exclusive ladies clubs but it also retained the harshness of the old west with its wildcat mining, unscrupulous dealings and the eventful arrival of troops sent by Theodore Roosevelt to quell a strike when the mines were consolidated.

This was Goldfield, the greatest and most flamboyant city in the state of Nevada.

By World War I gold production declined, businesses closed and many of its residents had left the area.

In 1913 a flash flood raged through Goldfield and ravaged the old brewery and red light district continuing on to destroy most of the town of Columbia. 1923 was the year a devastating fire consumed fifty-four city blocks reducing

Goldfield to scorched and blackened ruins. Although the fire had started in the Brown-Parker garage directly across the street from the Goldfield Hotel, the hotel escaped the conflagration unscathed.

By 1924 another smaller fire claimed several other buildings including the printing plant of the Goldfield Tribune, its one remaining newspaper still in circulation.

Little remains of Goldfield today although abandoned mine shafts, old headframes and miner's shacks can still be found in the distance, but only a few original buildings still stand as if in tribute to Goldfield's glorious past

North-west corner, Elliot & Euclid, Goldfield, Nevada. Winter, early 1981, looking West with Malapai mountains in the background. A typical original Goldfield house.

Goldfield's Courthouse and Fire Station still in use.

BUT YOU CAN'T LEAVE, SHIRLEY

Goodbye Nevada, Goodbye My Dream

PART I

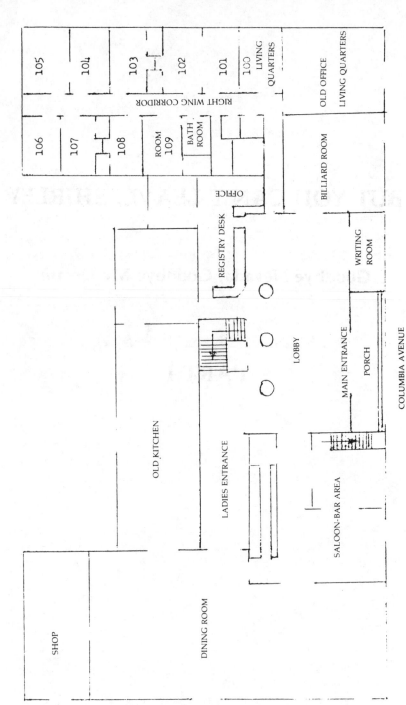

COLUMBIA AVENUE
GOLDFIELD HOTEL - MAIN FLOOR PLAN

Chapter One

From the moment I entered the room I felt the terror that was to haunt me during the next five years. I sensed it immediately; the cold, the hostility and an overpowering sense of fear. I stood there, temporarily unable to move, enveloped by cold chills and feeling an urgency to leave. What was it? What was in this room? I knew I had to leave, but at that moment I felt trapped as if being held back by some unseen power.

I didn't know if I could take the few short steps to the doorway that would lead me away from this living nightmare, but I had to try. With trembling hands, I grasped the doornob, pulling myself into the safety of the old corridor. Overcome with relief, I quickly closed the door, shutting away the horror that dwelt inside. I had made it. It was over.

Little did I know it was just the beginning.

Minutes before I entered this particular room I had set out to find several rooms suitable for living quarters in the old Goldfield Hotel which we had recently purchased. Due to water availability, the rooms would have to be situated in the right wing. The right wing, as it was called consisted of a vast hallway almost eighty-five feet long with fifteen doors opening into an office, guest rooms and bathroom facilities. The wing was used by the hired help when the hotel opened in 1908. The hall was narrower than the ones on the upper floors and with its fourteen foot high ceilings took on a cavernous look. Remnants of red plush carpeting still adhered to the floors, reminding one of the elegance the hotel enjoyed in its grandiose days. Transom windows had been left ajar in hopes of cooling the rooms although they had not seen any inhabitants for almost forty years.

I felt a sadness as I walked down the old corridor, so quiet and still, as if it had already taken its place in history.

1

As I opened the door to each room, I found that they were similiar in size and appearance and all showed the same signs of neglect. Most of the furnishings had been removed years ago, although long-unused radiators stood silently by. Peeling wallpaper nearly touched the dust covered floors and the tattered remains of window shades filtered slats of sunlight into the lonely vacant rooms. I had just about made the decision as to where we would set up housekeeping when I approached the last doorway. The brass numbers were no longer on the door but the outline remained, clearly showing this was room 109. Written in chalk that was fading but still visible, was the word "storage". It was here, in this room, that I encountered the fear that was to be with me all the years that I lived at the Goldfield Hotel.

I hurriedly ran into the lobby and rejoined my family. Dennis, my business partner and family friend, whom I later married, was unloading our belongings from the moving van. Lisa, my seventeen year old daughter, was frantically trying to locate her water bed, while dancing merrily around the circular settees was Mary Lynn, my fifteen year old who had been born mentally retarded. In this atmosphere I found myself wondering if I could have imagined the occurrence in the room and thought it best if I put it out of my mind. It had been a tedious trip through the mountains before we reached Goldfield and I was very tired. Still it was hard to rid myself of the feeling that something frightening was in that room.

I had to forget about that now. It was already late afternoon and beds had to be set up for sleeping, furniture arranged, and some of our clothing unpacked. It would be dark in a matter of hours and we did not have electricity to light up the hotel at night.

I had selected the two rooms that we would use temporarily, one of them being an old office. The office had been chosen as it was quite large and had two outer doors leading directly into the street. I felt more secure, knowing we could exit the hotel quickly if something unforseen was to occur. The hotel had been vacant for some time after the caretaker had moved away and many attempts had been made to break into the old building.

The next few hours were spent trying to make our new quarters livable. As Dennis moved the large pieces of furniture into place, I rummaged through packing crates to find draperies suitable to insure privacy and blankets that would ward off the evening chill. Lisa was busily upending boxes, strewing their contents on the lobby floor in search of decorative items that would bring brightness into the otherwise drab rooms.

I found some panels that would fit over the long narrow windows and was in the process of hanging them when I heard a loud thud that seemed to come from the center of the hotel.

I rushed into the lobby and found Lisa lying at the foot of the staircase, laughing hysterically, her small body encased in a mattress that was over seventy years old. Not having water for her waterbed, she was determined not to be deprived of a bed to sleep on that night. Barely five feet tall, she had managed to drag the old mattress down two flights of stairs when she promptly slid down the third. Standing by, surveying the situation, was Mary Lynn, trying to comprehend the humor of someone rolling down the stairs. It was beginning to feel like home.

I help Lisa pull the old mattress into the bedroom, where we laid it on top of an equally old iron spring that she had dredged up from God knows where. With a smug look of satisfaction on her face, she informed me she would decorate this room by herself. I returned to my drapery hanging, making sure the glass on the two front doors were also covered. This would help keep out the cold and the curious eyes of tourists.

With the exception of a few finishing touches, there was little to do in the old office. Lisa was still hard at work in the adjoining room and Dennis had set out for the nearest service station to fill our containers with water.

My next chore would be to find temporary sleeping quarters for our dogs Bruno, Dini, and Gabriel. As it became increasingly darker in the hotel, I decided to bed them down in the lobby. They were good watchdogs and I would feel more protected if they were nearby. As the dogs settled down for the night, I heard Lisa calling to me, "Mother, come look at the room".

I hurried through the dim hallway where Lisa was anxiously awaiting my opinion. As I looked around, I found it hard to believe this was the same room. Fresh plants were everywhere, pictures covered the cracked walls and brightly colored throw pillows were lying atop a cheerful bedspread. Everywhere I looked I saw a touch of home. Lisa had transformed this dreary, empty space into a warm, inviting bedroom. In these familiar surroundings, I began to feel more at ease in this section of the hotel, although it was just a short distance from Room 109.

By the time Dennis returned, the sun had disappeared over the Malapai Mountains and we knew we had to light our kerosene lamps before we found ourselves in total darkness. As we lit the lamps, we placed candles and flashlights next to each bed to be used if we had occasion to enter the main section of the hotel. It was becoming quite cold in the hotel as the desert winds began sweeping through the cracks of the front door and we all agreed the best place to be was under the mounds of blankets that covered our beds. After a light supper of sandwiches and milk, we wrapped ourselves in warm robes and crawled into our beds looking forward to a well deserved rest.

It was then I realized I had forgotten to lock the main entries.

Lisa and I each took a flashlight and entered the small hallway that would lead us into the lobby. As I passed the registry desk, I glanced over my shoulder at the staircase making sure we were the only ones there. Casting the beam of light on the floor, we made our way to the front door where we locked them without delay. Now we had to check the doors in the saloon and dining room which were equally as dark. Remembering where I had left the dogs, I called out, "Bruno, Dino, Gabriel", and all three came rushing to my side. We felt much safer now and it took only a few minutes to secure the rest of the building and return to the bedroom.

As I opened the door to the bedroom, I took one last look down the old corridor, lit only by the reflection of our oil lamps. I found myself staring at the door that led into the room that had terrified me earlier in the day. It was still there. It wasn't my imagination. Whatever it was seemed to be hovering over the doorway as if inviting me to come in. With a shudder, I locked our door, closing us off from the rest of the hotel.

As I crawled into bed, I pushed these strange feelings from my mind turning my thoughts back to the day I first saw Goldfield.

Goldfield High School built in 1905 and was the most elegant High School in the State of Nevada when it was built. The building is still standing.

Chapter Two

I first saw the hotel over twenty years ago in 1959. It was a hot August day and the last day of our vacation. My husband and I had decided to spend this day showing our children Nevada's old mining camps.

After miles of barren desert, I saw ahead of us a town, a town I would never forget. It was perfect, it was beautiful. This was it. This is what I wanted my children to see. At first it appeared deserted as I could see no signs of life. Dust covered streets and a few old buildings made up the main street. We took a turn off the main highway and found ourselves surrounded by memories of the past. Old miner's shacks, banks, saloons, skeletons of mining operations. I loved it all, the wind, the dust, the feeling I had of being there when it all began. This was truly the beginning of Nevada.

And then I saw her. This beautiful old building standing proudly among the ruins of what was once a great Nevada city. I couldn't believe that in the middle of this windswept desert that anyone could erect a structure such as this. Four stories of solid brick, balconies overhanging a columned porch and massive front doors leading into a gold ceilinged lobby.

I wanted to open those huge doors and walk into the past, but the "NO TRESPASSING" signs kept me at a distance as I stood in awe of her. I felt fortunate. We had seen a great monument to Nevada's gold mining past. This was original, this was history. I never forgot her, I never forgot the town.

Years passed and circumstances changed. Three of my children were grown. My family now consisted of myself and two daughters, one a teenager of fifteen, the other born mentally retarded with Down's Syndrome. Where money had not been a problem before, it was now a day to day struggle to keep a home together as their father was gone.

Unlike other teenagers who looked forward to recreation after school, my daughter joined me in cleaning vacated apartments, our way of earning a living. I would look at my daughter kneeling beside me cleaning floors and promised her that somehow I would make it up to her. She never complained and I doubt she ever really believed I would find a way to make life easier.

Determination can work miracles, however, and my mind never stopped working on a way to start a small business of our own. Two years later after a series of unsuccessful ventures, we found one of our handcrafted items were very much in demand. By this time we had a partner, Dennis, so we started a small business in our home. I couldn't believe what was happening. Everyone seemed to want our product. Orders were endless. We worked twenty hours a day to fill them. We had to open a retail store to service our customers. Gone were the years of cleaning apartments, baby sitting and taking in ironing to support my family. We were on the way. I had kept my promise to my daughter.

At this point our lives took another drastic change. We were to attend a gift buying show in Las Vegas to purchase stock for our retail store. It was decided that we would drive to the convention so Dennis and Lisa could see this town that had never left my memory. It was June 20, 1976.

I never realized how much I missed the desert until I saw it again. It was good to be back in this part of Nevada. I was anxious. Every mountain, every shrub, every turn in the road brought me closer to my town. Would the building still be there? Had someone torn it down? I had told them so much about it that it had to be there. Five hours later we rounded the last bend that brought me back to my memory. With only five miles to go, I strained to see the outline of the town. It was there. This huge structure loomed before me and even at a distance, I knew it was her.

I parked the car and we literally ran to the front door. I looked in. Everyone was in agreement. This was the most beautiful building ever to be built in the middle of the desert. I couldn't believe I was seeing her again. It was like coming home.

But what had they done to her through the years? The furniture was no longer there, boards replaced broken windows, peeling paint and crumbling cement gave credence to her neglect.

I was angry. How could anyone let this historical old building get into a state of decay? This was part of Nevada's history. Who had the right to do this.?

Then I saw it. A 16 x 20 inch piece of metal that was to be the beginning and end of our dream. A simple "For Sale" sign that would take away my faith in humanity and to deprive so many others of their opportunity in life.

The sign carried the name of a Las Vegas broker. I would contact him later. Could we afford it? I had to try. Someone had to care for this building.

Several hours later, we checked into a Las Vegas hotel and after unpacking our luggage, I placed a call to the realty office. I set up an appointment to inspect the interior of the building later in the week after we had concluded our business at the convention center. We were all so anxious to see the inside of the hotel however that the following day found us driving the two hundred miles back to Goldfield with the broker.

Upon our arrival, he led us up the crumbling steps to the porch covered with mosaic marble tile, some of which spelled out the words "Goldfield Hotel". We waited impatiently while he fumbled with the keys, trying to find the right one that would open the padlock on the huge doors. At last we heard the click of the lock and he pushed the door open, allowing us to enter.

"Oh Dennis, it's beautiful". "Oh Lisa, isn't it beautiful?" After over twenty years, I was finally standing in the lobby of the Goldfield Hotel and, indeed, she looked beautiful to me.

I walked over to the registry desk, built at the turn of the century of solid mahogany, then to the telephone switchboard directly behind it. I looked at the old wall safe, filing cabinets, and the mail pigeonholes with aging letters still in the slots.

Lobby of the famed Goldfield Hotel on opening Day, January 18, 1908.

Dennis called me from the saloon, "Come look at the bar", while Lisa's voice coming from the top of the stairs, was urging me to "come up and look at the rooms".

I wanted to see everything, the elevator cage with its brass doors, the black leather settees wound around the stately pillars, the clawfoot tubs, just everything. We were unable to see the entire hotel as the broker was on a time schedule and we had yet to view the additional properties being sold along with the hotel. But I had seen enough to know that somehow we had to buy this building and care for it. The rooms were littered with debris, mounds of broken glass covered the floors, and water trickled down the walls from a roof badly in need of repair. Everywhere I looked I saw the signs of years of neglect, but still, this grand old hostelry looked beautiful to me.

We returned to Las Vegas and four days later, we were on our way back to California. All of the conversation on the trip centered around the purchase of the hotel. Upon our return, we began negotiations and sent a substantial amount of money to the realtor. We reached an agreement and waited for our legal papers to come through the mail.

During this time we made several trips to Goldfield to visit the hotel. There was nothing frightening about the building but I always had the feeling that we were not alone. It was as if the hotel had a soul of its own. I told Dennis repeatedly that this old building held a secret and at that time I felt it had something to do with the basement.

We were unable to spend more than a few hours in Goldfield on these visits as we could not spare the time away from our business in California. On one occasion we made arrangements to stay overnight in the hotel with friends and several members of my family. It was that particular night that I had to admit, that something or someone was haunting the Goldfield Hotel.

Dennis and I, along with Mary Lynn and Lisa, set out for Goldfield early in the morning. Lisa's friend Jim, who was studying to become a minister, was to meet us there on his way from Yosemite. Susan, my oldest daughter, and her husband Michael would join us at the hotel by early afternoon.

As we were the first ones to arrive, we hauled old mattresses down from the third floor and laid them side by side in an alcove off the lobby known as the writing room. We covered the mattresses with blankets we had brought with us and dusted the registry desk and settees in preparation for our guests. Dennis had brought along our hobnail oil lamp of ruby glass and crystal and set it upon the seventy year old grand piano. It would not only bring a touch of elegance back into the hotel but it would give us sufficient light during the evening hours.

Jim was the first to arrive and Lisa took him on a tour of the hotel and the town while Dennis and I finished cleaning the lobby. By the time Susan and Michael arrived, the Goldfield Hotel was ready to welcome its first guests in many years.

As Susan stepped from the van, she was followed by Sally, a young girl of nineteen who was a frequent visitor to our shop in California. Upon showing interest in our newly acquired property, we had invited her to join us on our overnight excursion.

After giving a grand tour of the hotel to our new arrivals, we were rejoined by Lisa and Jim, who promptly invited Susan and Michael to ride with them in search of ruins from Goldfield's past. This left us to entertain Sally.

We spent most of the afternoon taking her for a walk through the streets of Goldfield, showing her the remnants of this once great city. We then took her to the old drug store where antique glass counters held a vast array of cold creams and home remedies from the early 1900's and then on to the small grocery store with its pot bellied stove so typical of that era. Mary Lynn's legs had begun to tire after our long walk, so we returned to the hotel, leaving Sally selecting necklaces at a collectible shop on the main street.

Dennis set up a makeshift table while I filled platters with cold meats and cheeses, anticipating the hunger of my offspring when they returned from their desert sojurn. Sally came bouncing through the lobby door, clutching her newly purchased treasures and immediately offered her help in preparing our picnic supper.

Moments later I heard the sound of Jim's van as it pulled up to the curb and I was relieved to see they had made it back to the hotel before dark. They were as hungry as I had suspected they would be and as I made platefuls of sandwiches, I listened to the stories of their ventures into the desert. They had seen old mineshafts, deserted buildings and had found ruins of a settlement near the first gold mining site, a town called Columbia. Lisa told of uncovering an early day dish, completely intact, only to break it while placing it into the van. Our conversation continued as we walked onto the porch and sat on the steps of the old hotel. It was quiet in the desert at night, the only sounds were from an occasional car traveling the highway and the echo of a tinkling piano coming from a nearby tavern.

Michael stood up abruptly and announced that he and Susan were going to Tonopah, a larger town twenty-six miles north of Goldfield. I whispered to Susan, "Aren't you going to stay here with us? I thought you were going to sleep here tonight". "Mother", she replied, "We'll only be gone a few hours, we'll be back later to sleep in the hotel". I felt a disappointment at her leaving. I not only would miss my daughter's company, but I had felt more secure knowing that she and Michael would be staying with us.

As Susan left for Tonopah, I thought about her reaction when she first entered the lobby, seeing it for the first time. "Mother, it's so big", she screamed. I reminded her that I had told her of its size when we first purchased the property. "I know, I know", she said. "but it's so big".

It was quite large, almost sixty-five feet long and forty-five feet in width. It resembled a huge ballroom, its floors covered with small marble tiles imported from Italy in 1907. It was in the alcove of this lobby that we were to spend the night. I was not overly concerned about sleeping overnight in the hotel, but it did have all the elements of a haunted house mystery and I had never stayed in the hotel after dark.

The desert winds came up suddenly bringing a blast of cold air into Goldfield and we hurriedly left the porch, seeking warmth in the hotel. Upon entering, we found to our dismay, that it was as cold inside the building as it had been outdoors. We bundled ourselves in additional clothing and crawled under the blankets that covered the mattresses on the alcove floor. Dennis blew out the wick on the oil lamp and we found ourselves in darkness, our only light coming from a lone street lamp on the main highway. I had just gotten myself into a comfortable position when I heard a strange rattling sound coming from the billiard room.

This room adjoined the lobby but was separated by two massive sliding doors, which had been left slightly open. At the turn of the century it had played host to male patrons only, and two mahogany framed glass doors led into the street, eliminating the need to enter through the hotel. The enormous windows were painted green, thereby insuring privacy in the event that some of the ladies of the town would be tempted to peek in and observe the men drinking at the bar or playing pool. Gentlemen of that era protected the ladies from the harshness of a man's world and resented their intrusion upon it. The room now stood hollow and empty, having been stripped of its furnishings years before.

I heard the noise again, this time there was creaking and a loud banging sound. I knew I would not be able to rest easily until I found the cause of these disturbances, so I took my flashlight and nervously stepped into the old billiard room. I stood there quietly and listened. It seemed to be coming from the outer wall near the boarded up windows. As I got closer, I found it was only the wind pounding against a loose board, causing it to flap against the window frames. Satisfied with this discovery, which also accounted for the creaking in the room, I returned to the comfort of my warm bedding, feeling very relieved.

We spent the next few hours talking amongst ourselves and firmly trying to convince Sally that spiders would not creep over her mattress and devour her body, a fear she had expressed many times during the evening. Sally's apprehensions would send Lisa into fits of laughter, echoed by Mary Lynn, and I would have to pull the covers over my head in order to regain my composure. It was an enjoyable evening and the furthest thought from my mind was fear of staying in the hotel.

We were planning on staying awake until Susan and Michael returned from Tonopah, but it was nearly midnight and we all agreed it was time for us to get some sleep.

We had been sleeping for several hours when I heard Dennis get up and saw him reach for the flashlight. The front door had opened and he needed light to lead Susan and her husband into the alcove. I heard him whisper, "Your daughter is home", as he walked to the doorway. I sat up, expecting to hear my daughter's voice, but instead I was greeted by silence.

Dennis returned to the alcove, saying, "I heard that door open, but there's no one there and the door is still closed,"

It was unmistakably the front door. The brass hinges had become very worn after more than seventy years of use and the door had settled to the floor, causing a harsh, grating noise whenever it was opened.

I wondered if it was possible that Susan had started to come in and then changed her mind, but her van was nowhere in sight. I didn't discuss the situation any further with Dennis, as I was trying not to disturb the others and cause them to become alarmed. I laid there quietly and tried to get back to sleep. A few minutes later a horrible, loud scraping sound came from the stairway as if someone was dragging a huge piece of metal down the steps. Somebody was in this hotel! Someone had to be in here with us! That's why we heard the door opening! Who was it and what did they want? All these thoughts raced through my mind as I laid there not uttering a sound. No one else had said a word so I assumed they were all sleeping. At last I heard Dennis ask very quietly, "Did you hear it?" "Yes, I heard it", I answered. We were soon joined by three other voices in repetition, saying "I heard it, I heard it, I heard it." Jim, Lisa and Sally had all been lying there awake, although each of them believed the others to be sleeping. We had all been aware of the strange sounds in the hotel, but it seemed as though no one wanted to admit it, as if by doing so we would have to accept the fact that someone was in the building. Instead, we laid there motionless, cowering under the covers. It struck me as being very funny and we all ended up laughing nervously about it.

The scraping continued. Someone was definitely in the lobby. I grabbed the flashlight and centered the beam on the staircase, checking each step and the landing, but no one was there. I directed the light towards the elevator, the registry desk and the circular settees, but found no one. Jim and Dennis got up and began to search the building. They walked from the lobby into the saloon and then on to the dining room, but found nothing unusual.

We laid back on our mattresses and for a short time it was quiet in the hotel. Jim, being a biblical student, insisted it was an intruder that was probably in hiding on one of the upper floors. I was beginning to believe that whoever it was, was not of our world.

And then it started, strange eerie noises were coming from the stairway, the old saloon and every part of the lobby. Sounds beyond description. We huddled in terror, waiting for them to stop, and finally . . . silence.

It was then I heard the footsteps walking directly at the

foot of my mattress and sounding like the shuffling of an old man's feet. I turned on the flashlight and looked down at the floor, dreading what I might see. But there was absolutely nothing there.

I turned to Jim. "How do you explain that? I told you it wasn't anything alive."

Jim finally agreed and walked to the stairway. As he ascended each step, he banged on the walls, yelling "Jesus! Jesus! Jesus!"

"Jim, come back", I screamed. "Get back here now!" He was not only making the situation more frightening, but I felt he would be in danger if he reached the second floor. Lisa pleaded with him to come back and he soon returned to the alcove.

I was tired of being intimidated by whatever was in the hotel and I boldly announced that I would cross the lobby, open the front door and release us from this ghostly tirade. We could sleep in our vehicles until daylight and then leave for home.

I never made it to the door. As I appoached the grand piano, I heard a sound that sent me scurrying back to my bed. It sounded like a tin cup falling off the bar onto the floor of the vacant saloon.

I was determined to try again. We had to get out of the building. As I neared the piano for the second time, I found I could not walk beyond it. I couldn't take another step. Something was holding me back. Was it fear, or something worse?

Whatever it was, I realized we were trapped in the lobby of the Goldfield Hotel, and I retreated to my mattress once again.

I looked out the window praying for dawn. "God, please let it be daylight", although I knew it would be dark for at least two more hours.

A hush came over the lobby, Mary Lynn had slept through the clamor and was resting peacefully. Sally was still hiding under her blankets and Jim and Lisa were carrying on a whispered conversation. The noises had subsided and we were all quietly discussing what to do in preparation for the next onslaught. I had to admit that it was something supernatural, a ghost from Goldfield's past, although my mind rebelled against such strange thoughts. But it was the only logical answer.

What had we done to this entity? Did it resent our intrusion upon its residence? Had we somehow invoked its spirit to return?

And then I remembered. It had seemed so immaterial at the time that I quickly dismissed it from my mind. It was earlier in the evening before I retired for the night. I was sitting on the leather settee thinking about the size of the dining room. In the past several months we had researched the hotel's background, reading all the available material we could find on the contractor and architect, and the names and characters of the men who had put the project together. The men instrumental in erecting the Goldfield Hotel.

There was one man I read about with interest, the man I called Mr. G., who seemed to have had a great admiration for the building. It was that man I called upon early in the evening.

I had read many books on Nevada's ghost towns and in every article that pertained to the hotel, it described the dining room as having seating for four hundred guests. There was no possible way this room could hold that amount of people, and although it was seemingly unimportant, I felt I had to solve this minor puzzle.

I nonchalantly asked aloud, "Mr G., you helped build this hotel, how did you get four hundred people into the dining room?" Seconds later I found myself running into the dining room and rapping on the wall separating it from another equally large room. I called out to Dennis, "Come here and bring me some light."

Dennis came in and I said, "Look at this, I think it's a fake wall." Dennis knocked on the wall and then took the flashlight and beamed it down on the tiled floor. The tile had been set in a pattern to border the outer edges of the floor, but by this wall, they continued on under the baseboard. We went into the other room and checked the base of the reverse side of the wall and there we found the extension of the pattern. I now had my answer to the puzzle. It was definitely a fake wall. Later, we were to find that the wall had been erected when Goldfield's population began to decline and there was no longer any need for the spacious dining room. The smaller section was originally used for a drug store and in later years, as an extension of the bar.

I thought about this incident as I lay in the alcove searching for an explanation. Did this have anything to do with the frightening events that had just taken place? Was it possible that Mr. G. still roamed the halls of the hotel he loved so much?

I looked across the darkened lobby and pleaded, "Mr. G., if this is you, for God's sake, make a noise on the registry desk so that we can get some rest." A loud thud resounded from the registry desk and I turned to the others and said quietly, "Its over, you can go to sleep." I wasn't frightened any longer. Somehow Mr. G. wanted me to know he was here and this was his way of making his presence known. I didn't fully understand what he wanted of us but I was too exhausted to worry about it any longer.

We awakened the next morning to a warm sunlit day. We had intended to leave early in the morning, but Michael and Susan still had not returned and I suggested we delay our departure for several hours.

When everyone was dressed, we left a note on the door for Susan and drove to a local cafe at the edge of town to have breakfast. Most of the conversation in the restaurant centered around what had occurred in the lobby the previous evening. Sally was still terrified but the rest of us had come to accept the situation, although not fully understanding the reason behind it. We returned to the hotel and found that Susan and Michael had still not arrived. We decided to wait until noon but then we would have to leave in order to reach our home in California before dark.

By noon we were ready to leave. Our belongings were in the car, the hotel was locked and it was obvious that Susan and Michael were not coming back to Goldfield.

Nine hours later we arrived only to find my daughter and

her husband had been there since morning having left for California directly from Tonopah the night before.

The next six months were troubled ones. We were having extensive problems pertaining to the purchase of the hotel and these problems were seriously affecting my health. I cannot elaborate on all of the negative aspects of our business transactions but it is sufficient to say that the purchase agreement was not the same as it was when it was presented to us. To cite one example, the property was offered to us as a real estate package. This package consisted of the Goldfield Hotel, the original 1905 high school building, a turn-of-the-century mining office building and ninety eight lots, many of which contained structures and mining tailings.

Several weeks after we had made our initial cash investment we inadvertently discovered that sixty five of these lots had recently been sold. The realty agent, after confirming that the lots were being sold, told me "take it or leave it". This news was very upsetting, but we still wanted the old hotel so despite the fact that the ninety eight lots were a major factor in our financial planning, we proceeded with our plans to purchase. At one point however we were prepared to lose the money we had invested and try to forget about the property. I had made this decision after an emergency trip to our local hospital. Trying to save the property and the questionable conduct in the purchasing agreements had made me ill. At this stage I was prepared to drop all transactions. I called the realtor from my hospital room and informed him that I was throughly disgusted with him, the seller and their less than honest tactics. I also told him that I had made an appointment to see a smaller historical hotel in Eureka, Nevada which was listed for sale and that I was no longer interested in the Goldfield properties even though we would lose ten thousand dollars.

The day I returned home from the hospital we received a call from the realtor. Another offer. Bring more money and the property would be entered into escrow immediately. I had my misgivings. Let it be. The additional funds he was requesting was all that we had left. I felt very strongly that we should not pursue this matter any further, but Dennis pleaded with me to accept the offer and against my better judgement we left for Las Vegas to meet with the agent.

I drove throughout the night to keep our early appointment but I felt bitter resentment with each mile that I drove. I did not trust the broker or the seller and I was totally against conducting any more business with them.

When we arrived in Las Vegas, we immediately went to the broker's house where he maintained his office. It was five minutes to seven in the morning. Our appointment was for seven o'clock. Dennis went to his front door to announce our arrival and when he answered the door, he asked Dennis to wait until he was ready for us. Dennis returned to the car where we waited, anticipating a short delay. After an hour had passed, I was in a rage. "Dennis", I said, "if he doesn't open that door in the next two minutes, I'm heading this car back to California. I've taken all I'm going to take off of that man!". Unfortunately, at that very moment, the door to his home opened and he motioned to us to come in. The escrow papers were on the realtor's desk awaiting our signature and we were assured that with our initial $10,000 and the additional $15,000 certified check that I carried with me, that the escrow would be opened at the title company within the next hour. With this assurance we left his office and started on our return trip to California, secure in the knowledge that we would be the owners of the Goldfield properties along with a large mortgage.

We stopped in Goldfield on our way home staying only a few minutes as the wind was whipping ferociously through the little town and Lisa was having trouble staying on her feet. Clinging to the walls for support, we made our way to the front porch of the hotel and peered in the windows of our newly acquired building. This was the moment I had waited so long for and all of the past problems seemed to have disappeared and I felt that it had been worth all the trouble we had gone through and as we carefully made our way back to the car, I was at peace with the world. The struggle was over. The beautiful Goldfield Hotel was ours.

But it was not to be. After arriving home in California, we waited for our legal documents to come through the mail. They never came. After numerous calls and complaints to the realtor, we eventually received something from the seller. It was one sheet of paper, an "Option to Purchase" stating that all parties agreed to this transaction, but having a line for only one signature, his.

I immediately telephoned the realtor in Las Vegas demanding an explanation. "Why was I given an option to purchase, why were we not in escrow and where was our $25,000?" I wanted answers to my questions, not the feeble replies I received in return. "Well, the seller wanted it this way", he said, "and I don't know where the money is, so call the seller". This was the most intelligent reply I could get from a state licensed real estate broker? I was enraged but I realized it was futile to argue with him as I would only get more of his equally unintelligent remarks in return.

I then called the title company. They were aware of our names but they didn't have our money. I called the seller. "Where's our $25,000, you didn't honor our agreement, so where is our money?" His answer, "Don't worry about it, Shirley", I couldn't get any further information from him and I slammed down the phone in utter frustration.

I couldn't believe this was happening. Our cash investment had seemingly disappeared, we were not given title to our property and neither of the parties involved would give me any answers.

Desperate at this point, I contacted an attorney in Las Vegas and explained our situation to him. He promised to contact the broker and the seller to see if they would honor our previous agreements.

I had also written to Governor Callahan of Nevada and related our experiences to him. We received a personal reply in which he thanked us for attempting to purchase and restore the Goldfield Hotel and apologized for the actions of the broker. He also stated that if we were to come to Carson City that we should bring the matter to the attention of his State Attorney General. I was grateful for his response and for the fact that he cared.

The Las Vegas attorney had also responded and informed us that the seller had agreed to proceed with the escrow and that Dennis and I should bring $500.00 to his office the following day and he would then accompany us to the realtor's office, at which time all parties involved would drive to the title company where a legitimate escrow would be opened. The $500.00 was his fee for representing us during this transaction and I felt very confident knowing that we had legal counsel even though the realtor had warned us at our first meeting that if we engaged an attorney, the seller would "call the deal off".

We left for Las vegas that same evening and again I drove all night to keep our early appointment. Driving down the dark highway, I kept reliving the events of the past weeks and I was deeply worried about our future. I was also concerned about leaving California again, but this matter had to be settled. I couldn't afford any more time away from home as I had a new problem to contend with. When we had returned from our previous trip to Las Vegas, the landlord of our shop notified me that in our absence he had signed an agreement to rent the shop to a friend of his. As I still had over two months left on my lease and my intentions were to renew the lease, this news was devastating to me. We spent weeks searching for a new location that would be both suitable and affordable, but unfortunately there was nothing available in our area at the time and the end result was that we would be out of business in less than two months and our income would come to a temporary halt. So I was very anxious to reach Las Vegas, finalize the escrow and return to California to devote all of my time to finding another location for our business.

Dennis, Lisa and I arrived at the attorney's office on schedule and after a few minutes conversation during which we paid him his fee, we made arrangements to meet at the realtor's office.

The realty agent was very congenial as he ushered us into his office and I felt quite comfortable until he informed us that he wasn't aware that he was to proceed with the escrow. Upon hearing this, the attorney and I both insisted that the realtor telephone the seller in Beverly Hills, California. This he did in our presence, using an intercom so that all of us would be able to hear the conversation. When questioned, the seller said he had "changed his mind" and nothing we said would alter his decision.

I couldn't believe what I was hearing. What was I doing here? Where was this "deal" the attorney had supposedly made? I looked to the attorney for help. He stood up. "Never, in all of my years of practice have I ever had someone change their mind after I had a firm comittment, I took the gentleman at his word". He looked toward us, "I'm sorry, there's nothing I can do here", and he bid us goodbye and left the office. I turned on the realtor. "What is going on? I drove all the way here to open an escrow, it was all arranged by the attorney".

"I don't know anything about it", he said. "Besides, I opened an escrow weeks ago".

"But there's no money in it", I screamed, "and it's worthless". Then I lashed out at him, giving my opinion of his worth as a realtor. But knowing it was fruitless to argue the point, I ran from his office to my car to do what any other women would do under the circumstances to release my frustrations. Cry.

We were back in California and our situation was worsening. I was in a constant highly agitated state but I still had to function and I still had to find a solution to our problems, but every day it became increasingly more difficult to do so.

We were unable to locate another shop for our business and as time was running out on our present lease, we held a close-out sale and sold our stock at a drastic loss. Deprived of our income but still having obligations to meet, we were rapidly going downhill financially as trying to solve the problems on the property had taken all of our reserve funds. Although we had just cause to take legal action against the broker and the seller, we were unable to initiate a lawsuit as we could not afford the enormous retainer that attorneys had requested. I realized that we could not financially survive much longer in our present situation and that I had to do something about it.

We did have the purchase option granting us "ingress and egress" which allowed us access to the hotel and I also had the keys to all of the buildings involved. Remembering the letter from the Governor advising us to meet with the State Attorney General, I arrived at the only possible solution. We sold much of our household and personal belongings, rented a large trailer and packing it to its maximum capacity, we prepared to move into the Goldfield Hotel. There in Nevada on common ground, we would fight for our property.

We had to leave many things behind in the house that we called home and before leaving I took one last lingering look and wondered if we would ever be able to return. I was apprehensive as to what was ahead of us but this was our only available option. On May 17, 1977, it was time to leave. Susan, my eldest daughter and her husband Michael, towed our trailer with their van which also provided space for our dogs. Dennis and I, along with Lisa and Mary Lynn left in our car on our journey to Goldfield with Lisa clutching her bowl of pet fish.

It was this set of circumstances that led us to set up housekeeping in the right wing of the Goldfield Hotel. This was the reason I found myself trying to sleep in the old office that led into the ominous corridor.

Two of the original buildings left in Goldfield, Nevada. The building on the left is George Wingfield's deep mines mining building, built in 1905. The little one-story building at the left edge next to the mining building is the original telegraph office which reported, round by round, the 42 round Nelson-Gans fight of 1906. Next to the mining building is one of five bank buildings. Photo taken, late summer of 1981.

Chapter Three

"Mum, I'm hungry".

"Mary Lynn, go away. I'll be up in a minute". I opened my eyes and glanced at the clock. It was barely six o'clock in the morning and I was still very tired. I looked over at Lisa, curled up in her blankets, sound asleep, and felt a twinge of envy. I was not looking forward to leaving my warm bed and stepping out into the cold air of the hotel, but I knew Mary Lynn would not let me rest until she had her breakfast. Then came the realization that, without electricity, I could not make anything warm for her to eat.

I dragged myself out of bed and looked around for Dennis. I couldn't find him anywhere, so I assumed he had left the building in search of hot coffee.

I was beginning to have misgivings about moving to Goldfield. Here we were, in a cold hotel, huddled in two

Author and daughter getting warmth from the sunshine because it was too cold inside the hotel.

24

rooms without electricity, running water or bathroom facilities. The situation was not enhanced by the knowledge that beyond my bedroom door was a hallway that I was in dread of. I chided myself about my lack of pioneer spirit and walked over to where Lisa was still asleep. "Wake up, sunshine", I said "We're going out for breakfast". Lisa quickly crawled out from under the covers, apparently looking forward to her first day of living in Goldfield. She looked at me and said, "Mother, I heard footsteps in the hallway last night and I was really scared".

"Oh Lisa", I scolded her. "Whenever you hear anything strange, wake me up. Just say "Mother" and I'll hear you". I felt guilty, thinking about her lying there frightened in the dark and not wanting to disturb me. At that time I wished we were home.

Dennis came in looking refreshed and carrying a cup of hot coffee. He had washed up at the service station and told us of the owner's generous offer to use his restroom until we could obtain our own running water.

Lisa and I took Mary Lynn, along with soap and towels, and set out to take advantage of his hospitality and hot water. Afterwards, we had breakfast and returned to the hotel to begin the extensive chore of cleaning the building. It was to take us several weeks before the building would look presentable. Many days were spent in the dining room removing debris that had reached a height of over five feet. Everything had to be sorted so as not to discard anything that could be used in the hotel.

Truckloads of trash strewn throughout the rooms were taken to the dump site at the edge of town. Windows that had not seen water in years, were washed and shined. Hours were spent polishing brass, cleaning woodwork and removing the thirty-five years of dust that had accumulated in the hotel. Every counter dusted, every floor scrubbed and each small repair brought the building closer to its original state. We were beginning to recapture some of the elegance that surrounded the hotel when it was completed in 1907.

It had not been an easy task to clean the main floor as

water had to be brought into the building in buckets and our work was constantly being interrupted by tourists wanting to look inside.

We had full intentions of opening the hotel for tours but only after our work was completed. We would listen to their stories, however, and they would tell of passing through Goldfield many times and finding the hotel closed and peeking at the interior through the windows. I would feel sympathetic, remembering how I had felt years before, so we found ourselves showing scores of people throughout the building from the basement up to the fourth floor. At times these tours would take hours as we would relate to everyone the events surrounding Goldfield's glorious past.

We finally came to the realization that in order to complete our project we would have to lock all entries and post "Private Property" and "Do Not Disturb" signs on the windows and doors. This brought little relief upon the intrusions of our privacy. If we neglected to lock any of the doors that opened into the hotel, we would find tourists roaming through the hallways and rooms, including our personal living quarters. It was not unusual to encounter someone searching through the old safe where I kept cash and valuables, but I was surprised to find one elderly lady looking through a box of my personal business papers. If the doors had been locked, we would find them peering at us through every window on the lower floor. At times like this, I felt as though I was living in a giant fishbowl.

We finally resigned ourselves to the fact that the tourists were determined to see the interior, and not wanting to deny them the pleasure, we would stop our work and invite them to come in. Eventually, after many delays, the main sections of the hotel were cleaned and ready to be decorated.

Dennis salvaged a large section of the original red carpeting from the third floor and patiently tacked it to each step of the stairway. Lisa and I had found one pair of faded drapes still hanging in the dining room since the turn of the century and hung them on the large front window of the lobby. These touches of red along with our ruby glass oil lamp atop the piano brought color into this room that was dominated by dark mahogany panelling. We purchased an antique service bell and set it on the counter of the registry desk along with an old inkwell and ledgers from that era. We then placed a vintage trunk next to the elevator and potted palms on the floor. With the exception of the original writing desks and lounge chairs, the lobby began to look much as it had when the hotel first opened its doors seventy years ago.

Our next project was to restore the same appearance to the old saloon. It had been painted a light blue, a color most unsuitable for a bar room. I knew this was not the original paint and the room had undoubtedly been repainted many times over the course of the years. One day I sat in the saloon and stared at the walls, trying to decide what color to paint them.

It had to be brown, not just any brown, but a certain shade I had in my mind. I mixed together several cans of paint, which we had brought with us from California, and after several attempts, I finally obtained the desired shade. It was perfect. Lisa retrieved and old rickety ladder from the basement where Dennis was repairing an original poker table that he intended to set up in the gaming area of the saloon. I climbed up the old ladder and started to paint as Lisa polished the back bar and lined it with bottles dating back to the early days of Goldfield.

Suddenly we were interrupted by the sound of someone walking with a heavy step on the floor above the dining room, which was adjacent to the saloon.

I called out to my daughter. "Lisa, we've got tourists upstairs again". Lisa came out from the bar and followed me as I went upstairs to confront our uninvited guest. We walked down the hallway towards the seven room suite that was directly over the dining room ceiling, not meeting anyone on our way. We searched every room of the suite, checking closets, bathrooms and looking behind each door, but there was no one in sight. We continued on to the end of the corridor and looked into each room. They were all empty. After checking all the upper floors, we returned to the saloon, assured that we were the only ones in the building, but knowing that minutes before, someone had been walking overhead.

Lisa and I resumed painting the walls of the saloon and as we neared a small section near the back bar, we found we could not get our brushes close enough to paint it unless the back bar was moved slightly forward. It was impossible for us to move it as it was massive in size and held sixteen feet of original glass mirrors in its huge frame. Dennis was in the gaming area of the saloon, arranging poker chips and cards on the felt covered table he had repaired in the basement. I called out to him, requesting his help.

He managed to nudge the corner of the back bar a few inches away from the wall and this allowed us to see the original paint that covered the wall when they first set the bar into place in 1907.

I couldn't believe it. There it was. The same shade of brown I had envisioned as I sat in the saloon that day, the same brown we were now putting on the walls. It was identical. I congratulated myself on being so perceptive.

We then told Dennis in detail about the sounds coming from the dining room and our search for tourists. He shrugged off our words with indifference, not being impressed with our ghostly footsteps.

I was a little perturbed. I recognized footsteps when I heard them and I had become accustomed to the various natural sounds in the hotel. Many times when Dennis was upstairs, I could hear him walking on the floors of the rooms above me.

I was not mistaken. They were definitely the heavy footsteps of a man walking in the rooms above the dining room. That day in the saloon was the first day I heard the footsteps, but it was not to be the last.

Chapter Four

Dennis was in the basement. You could hear the reverberations of the water pipes as he worked on them, crouched in a small dark space under the flooring of the right wing. The pipes were old, but in fairly good condition considering they were the original ones dating back to the construction of the hotel. It was taking longer than he had anticipated as he had to crawl over rocks and mounds of dirt to clear and reconnect both sewer and water lines. The water had already been turned on at the main and we were elated at the prospect of having our own running water. Dennis had completed some of the work the day before and we now had bathroom facilities, but no water coming out of the faucets. Our bathroom was divided into two separate rooms, an arrangement very prevalent in hotels of that era. A private bath was a luxury in those days and in the Goldfield Hotel they could only be found in the large suites of rooms.

He was trying to bring water into the hotel as soon as possible, not only for our personal needs, but we had received word from our former neighbors in California that they were coming to Goldfield to spend several days with us in the hotel.

Dennis came up from the basement covered with dirt and proudly announced that we now had water. I was ecstatic. "Where?", I asked. "In the billiard room", he said, "It's the only place I could get a pipe through in a hurry". "The billiard room? What are we going to do with water in the billiard room?"

Dennis answered "Well, you wanted water right away", and led me into the room to show me his accomplishment. There it was. A three foot pipe standing next to an old radiator with an antique faucet connected to the top of it. It looked a little strange but we did have running water.

We now had to select a room and decorate it in preparation for our guests. Unfortunately, the only rooms to choose from were the ones in the old corridor. Lisa and I went from room to room trying to find the one in the best condition with all the windows intact, but not giving any consideration to 109.

We decided on the corner room at the far end of the hallway. It was sunny and bright and the glass panes were all in one piece. It also adjoined another room giving it a spacious open look. Most of the wallpaper had fallen away so it would be fairly easy to scrape off the remaining pieces and paint the room.

Lisa and I went on a search for paint, as we had used up the supply we had on hand. This was not something you could buy in Goldfield, but we finally located some at an antique shop. We didn't know what color it was as the cans were quite old and the labels were gone, but it was all we could find on short notice.

It was khaki, a horrible dull color. We had no choice, we had to use it and we kept reminding ourselves that at least it was clean. We washed the windows, cut off the ragged edges of the window shades and hung freshly washed yellow curtains on the brass rods. Dennis set up an old double bed, and Lisa covered it with linen and blankets, including a bright floral bedspread. We hung a mirror above the dresser that we had moved into the room and placed a vase of artificial flowers and several books on top of it. With the addition of a few more home-like touches, the room was ready for our guests who would be arriving in two days.

I awakened Lisa at six o'clock the next morning. "Come on, sunshine, we get to take a sponge bath in the hotel, no more service station". Lisa got up from her bed and after gathering her robe and some fresh clothing, followed me into the billiard room. Dennis had found two old galvanized wash tubs and had put them in the room near the water pipe. We filled the tubs with water and proceeded to take our baths. The water was very cold so I quickly bathed and slipped into my bathrobe. Lisa was still standing in the tub rinsing her legs with fresh water.

"Good morning!" I couldn't believe what I was hearing. There in the lobby, at 6:00 in the morning, stood two tourists, expecting me to greet them in return. As I covered Lisa with a robe, I wondered how long they had been there. I explained to them, as tactfully as I could at the moment, that this was our home, the signs were posted, and that I rarely received guests at this ungodly hour, especially when I was not dressed for the occasion.

It was that day that I decided to take Bruno, our trained watchdog, out of the backyard and let him run loose in the hotel, and from that time on we were always aware when someone was at the door.

After we dressed, we walked back toward the end of the corridor to the room we had prepared for Ray and Angela, our neighbors from California. Lisa and I sat on the edge of the bed discussing our ghost situation. I felt that we should inform them of the occurrence in the hallway, although I did not wish to alarm them and cast a pall on their stay. It was difficult to decide what to do.

I had never sensed anything unusual in this room and with its bright curtains and bedspread, there was nothing sinister about its appearance, but directly outside the door, that feeling of eeriness still prevailed throughout the entire hallway.

Lisa suggested not telling them, explaining that in all probability, they wouldn't even notice it and would sleep through any noises. "Besides," she added with her usual laugh, "they'll find out for themselves, anyway".

"Oh, Lisa", I said, "we can't do this to our friends".

It was too late to make other sleeping arrangements and Lisa was probably right, they wouldn't notice anything strange. Besides, the room did look somewhat cheerful, so I decided not to tell them.

The day passed quickly and the next morning found us sitting on the porch anxiously awaiting the arrival of our friends. After what seemed like hours, we finally saw their car pull up in front of the hotel and we ran out to greet them. It was good to see someone from home. There was Ray and Angela, their son Ray Jr., and someone else that I didn't recognize. Ray introduced us, the other person was Angela's mother.

I welcomed everyone into the hotel and Dennis helped carry their luggage into their room, where we explained to them that as we were not expecting her mother, we had not made any sleeping arrangements for her. We said we could set up another bed in the adjoining room, but the room was in poor condition.

Her mother answerd, "Set up a bed anywhere. I'm not fussy, I'll be fine, I'll sleep in here with my grandson".

With that matter taken care of, we were able to relax and enjoy the day with our friends. When evening came, we set up kerosene lamps in their room and retired for the night. I slept well, knowing that there would be four people sleeping in the room in case something should occur, and this helped relieve my feelings of guilt.

When I awoke in the morning, I found Angela was already brewing a pot of coffee on a Coleman stove they brought with them to Goldfield. She had set it up in the saloon and everyone was standing around talking while waiting for the coffee to perk. As I walked in, Ray came up to me and asked, "Shirley, what's in the room down there?"

"Uh, what do you mean?" I said, knowing full well what he was talking about.

"Well, when we first got into bed, we felt this coldness, I mean, really cold. Then all night we had the feeling that we weren't alone."

Angela interjected, "It was like someone was staring at us, I know somebody was there. I could almost feel their eyes looking down on us."

Her mother agreed, "Oh, there was somebody there, allright. You could just feel them".

They went on with their stories, telling of lying in their beds for hours, feeling those unseen presences, not being afraid, but definitely being aware that someone was in the room with them.

I had to tell them the truth. "The hallway's haunted", I said. "I didn't want to mention it as I felt it might upset you.

I'll change your room if you want me to. We can set up something in the lobby."

"You don't have to do that", Ray replied. "It doesn't bother us. We just want you to know that something's in the room. And you're right about the hallway, it does seem to come from there, I felt it as soon as I walked to the other end."

Ray was a strong, hardy man in his late thirties, not the type to imagine something like this, and by relating his experience, he substantiated the reasons for my fear of the corridor.

I had suspected that they would hear a few noises during the night, but I was totally unprepared for their encounter with these ghostly entities. What did they want with my friends? Did they resent them being there, or were they just curious? Whatever the answer, every day it became more difficult to accept the fact that they were here at all.

We spent the next two days entertaining Ray and his family and then it was time for them to leave. We had enjoyed their visit and regretted that they had to return to California, so with their promise to come back again, we reluctantly bid them goodbye.

Esmeralda County Court House, 1907

Chapter Five

With the completion of the saloon, we felt we would be able to open for tours in a short time. We had done everything possible to make the main floor of the hotel clean and inviting while retaining the flavor of the post Victorian era.

Our lives had become adjusted to living in the hotel and I had come to love the building and considered it our home.

Lisa had found a good friend in Goldfield, the daughter of the owners of the country grocery store. The store was across the street from us and being so close, she would spend hours in Lisa's bedroom and the sound of their laughter would echo through the spacious lobby.

Mary Lynn was content in her new environment and had made friends with several local residents. Knowing of her handicap, they would show her special kindnesses and I knew in Goldfield she was loved and protected.

At times I found it difficult to believe that I was actually living in this beautiful town in the middle of Nevada's desert. As a child growing up on the outskirts of Chicago, I longed to move to the west, although I had never been there before. Where there were clouds, I saw mountains, empty lots became open ranges, and I would envision myself on a moonlit night, listening to the howl of the coyotes. The dreams of my childhood had been realized. I was finally here and I felt very much at home.

Our evenings were spent on the pillared porch watching the lightening storms over Lone Mountain. The days would be warm and sunny, but late afternoon would bring the desert winds and, invariably, by early evening, lightening would appear in the distance.

Dennis would play his accordian and we would sit on the porch and sing to his accompaniment. Soon we were visited by some of the townspeople who would join us as we sang. Music had returned to the old building and every evening ended with the playing of hymns, my favorite "Mine eyes have seen the glory of the coming of the Lord. . . the Battle Hymn". We did have a battle ahead of us. We were not aware of it then, but it would be two years before we received title to the hotel.

We felt so much at home in the hotel that I was no longer afraid to walk through the building after dark. Dennis usually retired early in the evening but Lisa and I would stay awake for hours afterwards, usually sitting on the old front porch. It became our nightly routine to lock all the doors in the hotel and lead ourselves back to our room by flashlights. Many nights found us sitting in darkness on the wide window sills of the saloon or the dining room, watching the traffic on the highway. We had learned to expect strange noises and footsteps that we would frequently hear in the building and Lisa, remembering what I had told her on the first day we lived in the hotel, would often call out to me "Mother, I hear something." We would leave our beds and roam through the hotel, trying to locate the origin of these unusual sounds. On one such occasion, Lisa awakened me, saying "Mother, Mother, wake up. Those 'nice' people you let stay overnight are ripping us off." "Lisa," I answered sleepily, "they wouldn't do anything like that."

They were a nice couple, an older man and his wife who were realty brokers from southern California. Although we were not officially open for tours, we had welcomed them into the hotel when we noticed them looking through the lobby window.They told us they were intrigued by old hotels and would spend their vacations in historic cities and towns and spending the nights in the oldest hotels that were available. I explained that we could not accomodate them as the building had been closed to the public for years. They were satisfied to be taken on an extensive tour and later drove to Goldfield's only motel to reserve a room. A short time later, they returned and told us they intended to sleep in their small camper as the hotel did not have any vacancy. I shared their concern about traveling to the next town as the winds had almost reached gale proportions.

But I also realized that it would be very cold and windy in the camper. As they left, I entertained the idea of letting them stay in the lobby on a spare iron bed, but feeling they were used to more comfort, I was too embarrassed to ask them. As if reading my mind, the woman abruptly turned from the camper door and re-entered the hotel. "Could we please throw our sleeping bags on the lobby floor and stay here for the night", she pleaded.

I assured her that she and her husband were very welcome and that we would be more than willing to set up the spare bed. We spent an enjoyable evening with them before retiring for the night.

I found it hard to believe what Lisa was saying. "Listen, Mother, you can hear them." I got up and stood by the doorway. I heard the sound of more than one person walking around the lobby as if they were moving things from one place to another. I wondered if they had become frightened during the night and were hurriedly packing to get out of the hotel as soon as possible. Lisa stood behind me in the dark hallway and followed my path as I proceeded to enter the lobby. Suddenly, the door leading to the main basement stairway began to rattle, sounding as if someone was trying to turn the doorknob while the slide lock was in place.

I whispered to Lisa "Why are they trying to get into the basement?" Their bed was only a few feet from the basement door at the far end of the lobby, but we were unable to see that far in the darkness. We tiptoed through the lobby and when we were halfway across, the noises stopped. We stood very still, not making a sound and then continued on the direction of their bed.

They were asleep, Deeply and soundly, wrapped in their sleeping bags and extra blankets which we had given them, their small suitcase still lying on the floor where they had placed it the night before. I assumed they had been so tired from the previous day's trip that they had slept through the clamor, and not wishing to awaken them, we walked quietly back to our room.

I said to my daughter "Lisa, this is getting ridiculous, we

are never going to get any sleep." "I know, Mother," she replied. "I don't like sleeping down at this end, I'm always waking up and hearing those noises in the hallway." She was referring to the old corridor. Fortunately, we did not have occasion to use it very often. To reach our rooms we would enter through a door on the right side of the lobby near the registry desk that led into a small hallway. This hall ended at the entrance to our living quarters, but continued on to the left for over eighty-five feet, thus making it the right wing of the U shaped building.

Lisa was very much aware of the strange aura surrounding this section of the hotel and although we avoided it as much as possible, she could not help hearing the sounds that emitted from the old passageway as she lay in her bed at night.

I worried about this brave little spirit who was always at her Mother's side as we roamed through the darkness of the hotel, and I tried to think of a way to ease the situation, not knowing at the time that it was soon to become much worse.

Nixon Block, Vermelyea, Edmonds and Stanley, Lawyers. Sanders and Swallow, Lawyers

Chapter Six

We opened the hotel for tours. Dennis had painted a large sign and placed it in the window of the dining room where it could be seen by tourists traveling through Goldfield. We were also setting up a small shop in the building, using some of the stock left over from our California store that we had recently closed. We added stacks of old newspapers and magazines, some of which we found in the hotel and the rest from my private collection. Along with our personal collectable items, we purchased some fairly antique pieces for resale as we did not have an over-abundance of merchandise.

My sister Darlene, who lived in nearby Lathrop Wells, heard of our plans to open the shop, and generously offered us the contents of a quonset hut on her property that at one time was used for an antique store.

Sister Darlene from Lathrop Wells, Nevada.

She and her husband owned a large business that was only ninety miles south of Goldfield. She explained that she was much too busy to sort through everything in the quonset hut as they not only operated the truck stop and bar, but also ran the restaurant, grocery store and trailer court. There was little time in her schedule to rummage through the hut, so she told us we were welcome to salvage anything that we considered saleable.

We made the short trip to Lathrop Wells, and returned with our car packed with relics from the past, including old wall clocks and a silver pocketwatch. With this addition of our newly acquired treasures, we were now able to open our shop.

Life in the hotel became very hectic during the next two months. Tourists noticed the "Open for Tours" sign that Dennis had placed in the window, and we were besieged with requests to view the inside of the building. We never knew when to expect them. Early morning travelers would knock on our door at dawn, while others driving through Goldfield in the evening, would insist upon seeing the hotel regardless of the fact that our only light came from kerosene lamps and flashlights.

The tours kept us very busy. Dennis was working on bringing electricity into the rooms, making repairs and cleaning the upper floors. If more than one group of people appeared at the door at the same time, he interrupted his work and showed them through the building. I was giving tours, but also running the shop with the help of my daughter Lisa. The only problem with this arrangement was that Lisa kept disappearing. I would return from a tour only to find the shop unattended as she had left to visit friends.

I told her, "Lisa, I can't be everywhere at once. I know you want to see your friends, but you can't leave the store alone. Bring your friends over here and visit with them while you wait for customers. If I'm not busy, then you can go out to see them."

We moved an old booth into the corner of the shop, which was located in the dining room. Here she could sit with her friends and serve them lunch or cold drinks, while engaging in typical teenage conversation. This helped ease the situation. Lisa still disappeared but not quite as often.

One day I walked in and found Lisa talking to one of her friends, who was the son of a local deputy with the Sheriff's department. She was telling him about the ghost that roamed throughout the hotel. I heard him say "they don't scare me, why, I'd sleep on the fourth floor all alone."

"Jeff," I said, "there are bats on the fourth floor, the ceiling is falling down, it's unsafe, and besides, it's very dark up there. I won't even go up to the fourth floor after dark."

He boasted of his bravery and insisted he was going to sleep on the fourth floor that night.

Again, "Jeff, you are not sleeping up there tonight. You would be up there all alone, something would frighten you, then you would run downstairs very fast, trip and break your neck on the steps. There will be no fourth floor for you."

Jeff grumbled, "What about the lobby?"

I agreed to him sleeping in the lobby if he had his father's permission. I warned him "If you sleep in the lobby, you may hear noises, something tries to open the basement door, so don't come complaining to me when you hear them."

Jeff received permission from his father to stay one night and we set up the old iron bed in the lobby. Lisa decided she wanted to keep him company, which meant that Mother would be there too. Dennis brought down another bed from upstairs so Lisa and I would have a place to sleep.

I was not looking forward to spending the night in the lobby, but I could not let Jeff sleep out there alone. Lisa crawled into bed with me, carrying her usual flashlight. I had Jeff move his bed close to ours in case he became frightened during the night.

They talked for hours while I laid there wishing they would fall asleep. Lisa was accustomed to the darkness of the lobby, and being in a playful mood, decided to make things more interesting for Jeff. She took her flashlight and sent the beam up the stairs, across the ceiling and anywhere she thought it would create a ghostly atmosphere. She would tell him stories of the strange happenings in the hotel, and he would insist he could handle anything, that "nothing scared him at all," The more he boasted, the more stories she would tell. This went on for hours until they finally fell asleep.

It had to be around three o'clock in the morning. Someone was shaking my bed. It was Jeff. "Shirley! Shirley! Get up. Someone's trying to open the basement door. Hurry, get up."

I could hear the rattling, the same sound Lisa and I had heard before when something was trying to open the basement door leading into the lobby.

I was not going to get up. I was tired from staying up late. In fact, at that time I was tired of all these strange things happening in the hotel and besides I had tried to warn Jeff the day before.

"Jeff," I yelled, "be quiet and go to sleep, it's only the ghosts."

Jeff crawled back into bed just as Lisa sat up and started laughing. The noises had stopped and I pulled the covers over my head and tried to get back to sleep. As I lay there, I wondered, if I hadn't been so tired, would I have had the courage to open the basement door? . . . and if I had, what would have been on the other side?

Ford and Buick garage sign, B.P. Garage sign

Chapter Seven

It was a day for celebration. We now had electricity. As the original wiring in the hotel was unsafe to use, Dennis had purchased cables and connected them to a new electrical box. It had been duly inspected and the power turned on. The cables came from the dining room, through the saloon and lobby and ended at the small hall by the entrance to our living quarters.

Mary Lynn couldn't seem to understand what all the excitement was about, but to the rest of us, it meant a great improvement in our life style. We would have electric lights, Lisa could play her records on the stereo and I would be able to prepare home cooked meals. Dennis was now working on disconnecting the water pipes from the billiard room and relocating them in the second section of our bathroom. This would give us running water in the sink and bathtub. By evening, we would be able to bathe in a

Helen Downing who, with her husband Grant, owned the Brown-Parker Garage while we were in Goldfield.

regular bathtub instead of using the antiquated laundry tubs.

I ran across the street to tell Helen and Grant about our having electricity. Helen and Grant Downing were are best friends in Goldfield. They owned the old Brown-Parker Garage which was directly across the street from the front of the hotel. It was now an antique shop, although they also carried a large supply of used merchandise. Old gas pumps, dating back to the nineteen twenties, stood in front of the building, still in service after more than fifty years. You could find just about anything you needed at the Brown-Parker and for travelers, Grant was an answer to their prayers.

Traveling Nevada's highways entailed many miles of barren desert between towns, and if a gas gauge read empty or mechanical difficulties arose, it meant being stranded for hours until help arrived. During late evening hours, the service stations were closed and help was unavailable. Almost nightly, I would hear the sound of a car pulling up in front of the old garage and Grant would get up from his bed to fill their tank with gas or do minor repairs.

Brown-Parker Garage in Goldfield, Nevada. Located across the street from the famous Goldfield Hotel. Built in 1904 and rebuilt in 1923 after the Goldfield's big fire. Photo taken in May, 1980. At that time the garage was owned by Grant & Helen Downing.

Many times, after being alerted by the Sheriff's department about a stranded motorist, you could hear Grant fire up his old tow truck on the way to give help, giving little concern to the interruption of his sleep.

Helen would work in the shop from early morning until dark, but still found time to raise fresh vegetables in her small garden, and care for her husband to whom she had been married for almost fifty years.

They made their living quarters in one section of their building and, to us, it was our second home. When I told them we had electricity, they were as excited as we were, since they shared so much of our lives. The only subject I didn't discuss with them was the haunting of the hotel. If I mentioned it, Grant would say, "There's no ghosts in there, I've been in there lots of times, I didn't see any ghosts." It was futile to argue with him, so I would let the matter drop.

I returned to the hotel as there were tourists waiting at my front door. I enjoyed giving tours as I loved to show people through the old hotel. I would inform them of the history of the building and Goldfield, as I led them from room to room. They delighted in standing behind the brass rail bar, holding up one of the dusty old bottles, while someone else in their group would take their picture. They would see the second floor, with its maze of three to seven room suites, and walk through the guest parlor that opened onto a balcony where they could view the town of Goldfield. From the balcony I would point out the ruins of what was once the main business district consisting of many fine banks, restaurants, elegant parlors, and the brewery along with the section that housed fifty-four bordellos, and tried to convey to them what Goldfield was like when it was the largest city in Nevada before it was destroyed by fire in 1923.

For the more adventurous tourists, I would take them to the fourth floor. This floor showed more damage, but it had more of an aura of the past than the floors below. It was also inhabited with bats, which did not seem to bother the tourists as I had warned them beforehand, but they did learn the art of ducking in a very short time.

We would then proceed to prowl around the basement. In 1907 the basement housed a large barber shop resplendent with mahogany framed bevelled mirrors and had a private entrance with an access from the main street. It also contained a lavatory for men only, which could be entered from the barber shop or from a separate stairway which led from the corner of the saloon area which was directly above this section of the basement. As women were not allowed in the saloon or barber shop, the open lavatory did not cause any problem.

In addition, there were two workshops, the boiler room, several smaller rooms, and next to the elevator machinery were the original electrical panels mounted on a marble base. Under the dining room area was a large room with an outside elevator and we presumed this space was used for bar and restaurant storage in Goldfield's early days.

In one corner there was a boarded up space on the floor. The real estate agent had informed me he felt it had to do with the plumbing system. It intriqued everyone as we were never quite sure of what was actually under the boards. It did add a touch of mystery, however, and the tourists loved the basement, although it had changed considerably throughout the years.

My tours would last for hours and I enjoyed them as much as our guests did, as I met such interesting people from politicians to carpenters alike.

Our day was soon over and we adjourned to our living quarters anxious to try out our new electrical outlets. Dennis had set up lamps in both of the rooms which gave a warm glow to our surroundings. Lisa was able to connect her stereo and several minutes later she and Mary Lynn were lying on her waterbed, enjoying her favorite records.

Water for hot coffee was bubbling in the pot while our first warm supper in the hotel was simmering on top of the hot plate. There was nothing sinister about our room and in this atmosphere there was a feeling of warmth and contentment. I had temporarily forgotten the terror that had gripped me so often, but I was not to forget much longer.

After dinner I decided to try out the bathtub that Dennis had reconnected earlier in the day. Unfortunately, the room that housed the tub was directly next to room 109 and as it was separated from the other bathroom facilities, I had never had an occasion to use it. It was, however, only a short distance from our living quarters and as our doors were open, I did not feel uncomfortable over the prospect of bathing in this room. We did not have electricity in the bathroom but Dennis had left an orange colored trouble light at the entrance of the old corridor. This was to be used to light our way through the halls at night and it gave off a rosy but dim glow. I hung the trouble light near the bathroom and, leaving the door open, returned to our living quarters to get the water I was heating for my bath, as the only water coming from the faucets was cold.

Lisa and Mary Lynn were still lying on the bed listening to records while Dennis was reading old papers that we had found in the hotel. In this calm, serene setting there wasn't any hint of what was to come.

Taking my robe and the hot water, I walked down the old corridor anxiously looking forward to stretching out in the tub as compared to crouching in the galvanized laundry buckets. The water was warm and relaxing. But within moments I began to have this feeling of uneasiness. This uneasiness soon turned to fear, the same fear I had experienced when I first entered the room next door.

What was it? Dear God, what was it? I became terrified. I called out, "Lisa, come here!" All I heard in return was the music coming from the room.

I tried to bathe quickly so I could leave but something began penetrating through my back as if laser beams were coursing through it. I glanced over my shoulder and saw only the front panel of the bathroom door which I had left open. It continued on. I sensed I was being stared at, as if someone was watching my every move.

I felt the piercing of my back again and whatever it was, was forcing me to turn around and look at the wall behind me. I was afraid and I didn't want to turn around but I was compelled to do so. I looked at the wall and screamed. "God, no!"

There it was, another door, almost hidden by the door I had left open. An adjoining door leading into room 109. With all my strength, I jumped from the tub, partially covered myself with my robe and ran into our living quarters, leaving modesty and a trail of soap suds behind me.

I ran to my daughter, "Lisa, Lisa. Didn't you hear me calling you?" I realized then that she couldn't hear me over the sound of the stereo. I explained to her what had happened and we decided that when one of us took a bath, the other one would stand close by.

That night we made plans to set up beds in the dining room. We would leave our bedrooms intact but we would sleep at the other end of the hotel.

Hunter's Department Store, 409 N. Columbia Avenue, July 4, 1908

Chapter Eight

Lisa, Mary Lynn and I were now sleeping in the dining room. Dennis prefered to sleep in the comfort of his bed in our old living quarters. He was not affected by the noises in that section of the hotel as he usually slept through the mysterious sounds and footsteps that prevailed throughout the old corridor. For Lisa and I it was a welcome relief to move from our bedrooms into the dining room.

It was a huge room with windows fronting Columbia Avenue and highway 95, giving us a sense of security we did not find in our rooms in the right wing.

Dennis had also set up a workshop in the center of the dining room and it was beginning to feel very comfortable. We had recently closed our shop as it had proven to be highly unprofitable and were now devoting most of our time to giving tours. Needing to increase our income, we decided to make check plaques to sell to our tourists.

We retrieved some tables from the original kitchen that I thought would be suitable for the work that needed to be done and had Dennis put them in the dining room along with the additional equipment and supplies that we would be using. Here we could work and sleep in an open area far removed from the opposite end of the building.

Dennis would cut the plaques and Lisa and I would glue a check from Goldfield's early mining days to the front of the plaques while the backs would carry a story of Goldfield's historic past. They were popular with the tourists, especially the Europeans that came by charter buses. Wanting a memento of their visit to Nevada, they found the check plaques convenient in size as they took very little space in their luggage and they also represented a small part of Nevada's fabulous mining era.

We would give our tours during daylight hours and by early evening we were ready to begin work on our check plaques. I was also preparing our meals in the saloon which was adjacent to the dining room and as we worked and slept in that area, we seldom ventured into the right wing.

If we were to use the bathroom facilities or needed something from our former bedroom, Lisa and I would accompany each other, never daring to enter that part of the hotel alone. We spent as little time as possible on these occasional trips to the right wing and would always hurry back to the safety of our new quarters. Since our new project was keeping us quite busy, we tried to give little thought to the strange sounds that emanated from that part of the building.

When our work on the plaques was finished for the evening, Dennis would retire to his room but Lisa and I would roll our bed in front of the screen doors of one of the side entries to the dining room. This gave us a full view of the highway and Goldfield's main street.

After turning off the lights, we would sit on top of our old iron bed for hours waiting for something unusual to occur that would interrupt the deathly stillness of the desert evening. Goldfield was like a ghost town during these late hours and the most excitement we found was watching the truckers gear down as they noticed the local deputy hiding in the shadows of a nearby service station.

Lisa could always find something humorous in the dullest of situations and some of my fondest memories of Goldfield are of the hours we spent talking and laughing until the wee hours of the morning while surveying the town from our old iron bed.

Three weeks had passed since we had first started work on our plaques and although I felt more at ease mentally in our present surroundings I was becoming greatly concerned over our continuing financial dilemma. We had been to Carson City and had met the State Attorney General's deputy in charge of real estate and he was shocked by our story. He telephoned the seller and demanded that he rectify the situation. We made an appointment to meet with the seller in Beverly Hills, California but as usual we did not have the funds available to initiate a lawsuit so we felt compelled to abide by what the seller proposed and the only new arrangements I could make with him involved another large sum of money to be paid in January. Years later when it was too late I discovered I had legal recourse other than a civil lawsuit.

I was very worried at this time and I sometimes deeply regretted leaving our home and business in California. I would think about our home and shop and wonder what we were doing in this hotel in the middle of this wind swept desert. We had only the simplest of modern conveniences, we seemed to be working constantly, preparing a meal was a major project using our antiquated equipment, and it was definitely a pioneer type of lifestyle. With all these draw-backs, we had the additional threat of losing our building in January. Still, we all knew we loved this grand old hotel which had become our home and we were perfectly willing to endure all of the hardships in order to keep her.

I realized the tours and plaques would not bring us the sum we needed in January, but I knew we had to raise enough capital to start up our business elsewhere before winter set in. With these thoughts in mind, I decided to work late every evening on our check plaques to raise additional funds.

On this one particular evening Lisa and Mary Lynn had bedded down early and were sound asleep well before midnight. I had been working on the plaques for hours and my thoughts were centered entirely upon the extra money I would be able to raise.

The dining room had a pleasant lived-in look, the girls were sleeping peacefully and I was not the least bit tired although it was almost 3:00 AM. But this quiet setting was soon to be interrupted.

I didn't pay attention to the footsteps at first, perhaps because they were unexpected and my thoughts were elsewhere. I felt my body stiffen as I came to the realization that I was actually hearing those footsteps, the same footsteps Lisa and I had heard the day we were cleaning the saloon.

I tried to ignore them, hoping they would go away, but it

continued on. I didn't want to awaken Lisa so I sat there gluing the checks on the plaques and pretending that I was not hearing anything unusual.

They became louder as if someone was stomping through the room above and I could no longer ignore them.

"Lisa, "I called quietly. "Lisa, they're back again."

Lisa sat up in her bed immediately. We huddled there, not making a sound, listening to the steps walking back and forth over a small section of the dining room ceiling.

It was at this time I became very angry. I was tired of being frightened, tired of my daughter being frightened, and just tired of all the unearthly occurrences in the building. Here we were, cowering in the dining room while the heavy thud of footsteps tromped above us and then I thought of Dennis sleeping uninterrupted in his bedroom. This made me even angrier. I had had enough of ghosts and noises and I was not about to subject myself or my children to this any longer, although Mary Lynn never became upset over these strange events.

It was time to wake up Dennis. I threw open the dining room doors, stormed through the darkened saloon into the lobby, then entered the old corridor leading to Dennis's

Door at right of picture leads into the hallway of the right wing.

room, all the time defying the spirits to make one unnerving sound.

"Dennis," I screamed, wakening him from his sleep. "If you don't come out to the dining room right now where that damn ghost is walking, I'm leaving this hotel and never coming back. I've had it, do you understand? I'm getting out of here and never coming back." After being assured he was fully awake, I retreated back to the dining room and my children.

Dennis came in shortly afterwards and I explained to him what had happened. I told him I wasn't thinking about ghosts while I was working, all of my thoughts were about earning money. I also told him I couldn't put up with this any longer and that if it happened again, we would leave the hotel.

Dennis listened to my tirade, but as he had not heard the footsteps, he was at a loss as to what to say. By this time the footsteps had ceased and we just sat quietly for awhile and then eventually fell asleep.

The next day Dennis moved another bed into the dining room and joined us in our new sleeping quarters.

Years later I came to realize that the spirit that roamed the rooms above the dining room always appeared when I needed help. But why? I was to find out all the answers later.

Chapter Nine

Summer was soon over and the cold desert winds blowing through the cracks of the doors gave us a fair warning that winter was coming to Goldfield. It was September and the chill had already crept into the old building. The tour buses no longer traveled the near deserted highway and only on rare occasions were we requested to give a tour of the hotel.

The hotel lobby which had hosted so many tourists during the summer season now sat idle and I knew it was time for us to leave.

Regardless of all the frightening experiences that we had endured during the past months, we still felt a reluctance to leave the hotel and the town that had become our home. We realized, however, that we would not be able to earn a living in Goldfield during the winter months let alone raise the capital we so desperately needed in January. In addition, we did not have any source of heat for the building except small electric heaters that would be totally inadequate for even a small portion of the hotel. Taking everything into consideration, we knew our only recourse was to move to a large area where we could reopen our business and live under normal conditions.

We were very unhappy over the prospect of leaving Goldfield but the thought of coming back in the spring when all legal matters were settled helped ease the pain of leaving.

It would take us several weeks to prepare for our move. Decisions had to be made as to what we would take with us and what we would leave behind.

At the end of two weeks we had finished our packing and found we had some spare time as the truck that was transporting our belongings was not due to leave Goldfield for at least ten days.

During this time Lisa and I decided to rummage through the basement to see if Dennis had overlooked anything when he removed our manufacturing equipment and tools. Whenever my daughter and I had prowled through the basement we would always find something old and intriguing. These became our treasures and we would leave them in the basement, usually in one of the maintenance rooms or next to the elevator machinery.

Feeling strongly that Dennis had not brought everything up from the basement, we then proceeded to check it out ourselves. We found a few things that he had neglected to take upstairs, items that were on the ground next to the elevator machinery. As we stood there I noticed some old pots and pans that were under the main stairway that led from the lobby to the basement. This stairway was next to the elevator shaft directly behind the machinery. It was warm in the basement compared to the upper floors and as we had nothing better to do with our time, we agreed the best thing to do was to find out just what was under the stairs. We were always willing to go on a scavenger hunt so we crawled under the stairway to see what "lost treasures" we could unearth. Using a flashlight we were able to find several other pots and kitchen utensils. Then Lisa found an old spoon.

Since the flooring under the stairs consisted mostly of dirt and what appeared to be crumbling concrete, she decided to dig with her new found spoon, hoping to find some rare artifact. Several minutes later she unearthed an old copper barrette which had turned green throughout the years. This piqued her interest and she decided to enlarge her search. Her tiny body was crouched under the bottom steps which was where she had found the barrette. By digging further, past the bottom step, she would be under the concrete walkway. This walkway started at the outer bottom step and led to all the rooms in the basement. After a few minutes she said, "Mother, look, I've found some bones." Not being an expert on the subject, I could not tell exactly what type of bones they were. She brought out several more that were fairly large and it appeared to me that they were human bones. It was then I decided to call the sheriff.

One of the deputies answered my call and when I showed him what Lisa had found he said, "Shirley, someone just buried a dog down here." I then explained to him that I thought someone had gone to a lot of trouble to bury a dog as the practice of earlier times was to use the backyard or the city dump. I could somewhat understand it if they had buried it under the stairway but the bones were found under the walkway beyond the stairs. Lisa had been working in a space no higher than eight inches when she found the bones and she had to lie on the floor to reach under the walkway. It did not seem plausible to me that anyone would take that means to bury a dog.

I asked him repeatedly if the bones could be from a small person or a child. He informed me it was a possibility but that there was nothing he could do about it. I reminded him that it was strange that the bones were not under the stairway floor where there was dirt and crumbling cement but were shoved under the walkway instead.

"Shirley," he said, "that's not old concrete, that's lime."

Now my curiosity was highly aroused as I knew why lime was used, although I did not have any idea what it looked like.

Shortly after the deputy left we were joined by one of Lisa's friends who wanted to continue the search for additional bones. Lisa was very upset after talking to the deputy and I thought it best to put an end to this project. I had never seen her as frightened as she was this day. She wanted to leave the basement immediately, so we gathered up our little treasures and the bones and went upstairs into the lobby. There I wrapped the bones in plastic, intending to bring them to a pathologist when we had occasion to be in Reno or Las Vegas.

I was still intrigued by the fact that someone had used lime to dispose of the bones. It appeared to me that whatever was buried there was of a fairly large size and when it was buried part of it was shoved under the walkway. The lime would destroy the portion under the floor but it could not reach the part under the concrete walkway, which would account for those bones being intact.

After this latest episode I was almost looking forward to leaving Goldfield. As much as I knew that Lisa loved the town and the hotel, I could not help feeling that this was not a normal way of life for a young girl. It seemed that everything we did turned into a horrifying experience, and this time it left her terribly upset.

The day came when our truck was loaded, the building secured, and we were on our way to Reno.

Chapter Ten

Upon our arrival in Reno we leased a large manufacturing shop and immediately began producing our product. The business started out successfully and all profits were set aside for the hotel. During this time we were also selling everything we had of value, but knowing the amount would be insufficient, we made arrangements for a loan. Unfortunately the loan was to be finalized two days after the date the money was due.

A letter came from the realtor. He informed us that we were to remove all of our belongings from the hotel. We asked the seller for a two day extension but the answer was a definite "No!", and now we were being told to vacate the building.

We knew we had cause for legal action but we could not find an attorney that would take our case.

We left for Goldfield shortly after receiving the letter from the real estate broker as we were given only a few days to remove our possessions from the hotel.

When we arrived at the hotel we found it was extremely cold and it was a difficult task to load the van under these conditions. It was even more difficult emotionally as we knew that we would never be able to live in our beautiful old building again. Many hours later we had the van filled to capacity and were ready to leave.

Before we left the hotel I walked into the saloon and stood behind the bar. I turned to Dennis who was standing beside me. "Dennis, what will they do to her now, turn her into a modern casino with slot machines all around, will anyone really take care of her? Damn!" I slammed my fist on the bar, and looking up at the ceiling, yelled, "Hotel, destroy yourself." I didn't really know who I was speaking to but I did know that something or someone also inhabited this hotel and I had a distinct feeling that someone was listening to me.

I left the saloon to go in search of my daughter who had been saying goodbye to her friends. I found her across the street in the old drug store. "Lisa, get in the van, it's getting dark and we have to leave. Tell your friends we'll be back in a day or two, we can't take everything on one trip."

As Lisa got into the van, Dennis locked up the hotel and soon we were on our way. I drove directly to Reno, stopping only for gas, and arrived at our shop close to midnight.

Two days later we were on our way back to Goldfield. I was not looking forward to this trip as I realized that this would be the last time I would see the hotel. I thought of all the plans we had made for the building and of the people that we had offered employment to. We wanted to hire the elderly, the handicapped and the unwanted. We had met so many of these people and knew they were very capable of helping us operate the hotel during and after restoration. It would now be their loss as well as ours.

We arrived in Goldfield by eleven o'clock in the morning and found that it was as cold as it was two days previously. Lisa decided to stay in the van where it was warmer but I followed Dennis into the hotel. I was in the lobby only a few minutes when I heard Dennis yelling in the saloon area. It was unlike him to do this and as I couldn't understand what he was saying, I ran into the saloon to find out what was happening. Dennis was standing in front of the bar looking as if he couldn't believe what he was seeing. The bar was warped, completely and utterly warped. It looked like a miniature roller coaster. There had not been any rainstorm that would have allowed water to drip onto the bar, in fact, we had been in the hotel during all kinds of weather but the bar had never warped. As I looked at it in disbelief, all I could say was, "Dennis, they heard me, they really heard me."

I walked into the dining room and there let out a scream of my own. The fake wall that divided the dining room had never been perfectly smooth but now it looked as if it was accordian pleated. In all the time we had been in the hotel it had never looked like this. I was beginning to wonder if the hotel was going to crumble to the ground brick by brick.

I walked back into the lobby preparing to move some things into the van. I went from room to room and gathered a few personal items that I wanted and put them by the front door. Although I had planned on spending hours removing everything of ours from the hotel, I suddenly found I could not stay there any longer.

"Dennis," I said, "just leave everything. I just want to get out of here." Dennis agreed and told me he'd be ready to leave in a few minutes. I then took one last walk through the old building.

I'll never forget the day we locked up the hotel knowing we would never see it again. It was very cold as I walked through the old corridors, reminiscing about how it had been in the summer. In the lobby the piano sat idle covered with dust. Gone was the ruby oil lamp that graced the top of the piano bringing color into the huge room. Gone were the sounds of voices singing to the accompaniment of Dennis' playing. I glanced at the hallway. Another memory. The main staircase had sat uncovered for years until Dennis had salvaged a seventy year old strip of carpeting from an upstairs hallway. He had worked for eight hours so each step would be perfect. A touch of red amongst the dark mahogany panelling. It had brightened the entire lobby and we were so proud of his accomplishment.

As I walked through the building every room became a memory and my resentment flared. What did the seller know or care about any of this? For years he had let the building decay. What did he know of us bringing our water in by the canful, or bathing in buckets, and of our little celebration when we had our own running water?

What did he know of the hours spent rewiring an old chandelier and installing new wiring or of the night we proudly turned on electric lights in the building after years of darkness?

My thoughts then turned to the fate of others, the elderly men that were to help plaster, paint and restore the building. What would they do now? They were to be a part of the hotel and part of our lives.

I couldn't look any more. This had been my home and the

one place in the world where I had wanted to spend the rest of my life. We had sacrificed everything we owned for the building and now it was all over, the hotel was lost to us.

I walked out of the hotel and got into our van. Inside Dennis played our theme song "Oh Dem Golden Slippers" on the dusty piano. Then he quietly hung the "Closed" sign on the front door and padlocked up our dream. For the last time I looked up at this building, which was not just a building to me. These four stories of brick and granite had a soul of its own. It held memories of the men who built Nevada, of happiness and tragedy, and business transactions that changed Nevada's history. It also held our laughter and tears. This was home, this was our dream and the dream of many others who were relying on us.

It was time to leave. Dennis stood by the door of the van looking up at the building. He had tears in his eyes. His only words, "Damn him, what does he care?"

I knew then I would have to leave Nevada. How could I stay here now? Every stretch of the desert would remind me of Goldfield. Every old mining shack, every old relic would remind me of home.

We started down the highway toward Reno and I told Lisa and Dennis not to look back, but I found myself glancing over my shoulder for one last look at the Goldfield Hotel and whispered to myself, "Goodbye Nevada, Goodby my dream."

It was January, 1978.

We were back in Reno. I wanted to leave the state immediately, hoping that this move would help ease the pain of losing the hotel. A move at this time however, would be impractical as we had taken many orders for our product and we had an obligation to our customers. It was also our source of income so we decided to stay and relocate at a later date. We then tried to attend to our business and put this part of our lives behind us, but it was very difficult and not a day went by that we did not discuss the hotel.

My thoughts were always of the hotel and I dwelled on it constantly. Why couldn't I just give it up and suffer the loss of the property? Even though I knew the property should have been ours legally and that we had lost financially, there was something more to it than that. It was the feeling that I had to go back to the hotel, it had to be part of my life.

When I would think about it realistically, I would chastise myself. Hadn't the hotel cost us our home and business in California, hadn't it caused the decline in my health, hadn't we given up enough for the building, and hadn't we endured enough hardships? I would also think about the spirits that inhabited the building. Did I really want to return and live in fear again? In spite of all this, I knew I had to go back, somehow I had to go back to the hotel.

But it was now a hopeless situation. I had recently met with several attorneys but none of them were willing to bring litigation against the parties involved. I finally resigned myself to the fact that I would never see the Goldfield Hotel again.

PART II
Oh! Dem Golden Slippers

Chapter Eleven

"Oh! Dem Golden Slippers, Oh! Dem Golden Slippers" The echo of the familiar refrain resounded throughout the lobby as Dennis played our theme song on the dusty old piano. As he lifted his fingers from the old ivory keys, he turned to me and jokingly asked, "How did we get back in here?"

"It wasn't easy, Dennis," I replied. "It wasn't easy but at least we're home."

It had been more than two years since we had locked up the old building, never expecting to see it again, and here we were standing in the lobby of the Goldfield Hotel, which once again was to be our home.

It was well after midnight and just minutes before entering the lobby we had parked our rented moving van on the deserted street in front of the hotel. It was March and the chill desert winds were whipping through Goldfield causing the hotel to be extremely cold.

After greeting the hotel with our theme song, Dennis and I now had to take one short trip to the truck to reteieve our dogs and some bedding that we would need for the night. It had been a long, tiring drive from Reno and all we wanted to do at this late hour was to get some sleep. We would unload the moving van in the morning.

Using the mattresses we had left in the dining room years ago, we set up temporary beds and covered them with layers of blankets because of the severe cold. The dogs were bedded down at the opposite end of the room with their own blankets which would keep them warm. I always felt more secure with my dogs nearby, but on this particular night I needed them to be close to me. Although we were accustomed to living in the hotel, it was still rather frightening to enter the building after dark when the hotel had been uninhabited for such a long time.

I had found myself looking over my shoulder as I walked from the lobby to the dining room as if expecting to see someone appear at one of the many doorways or from the open staircase that led from the basement into the darkened saloon.

These thoughts were not entirely imaginary as there was a possibility that a vagrant had somehow entered the building seeking shelter and was still living on the premises.

I was, however, in the safety of the dining room with its three exits and the dogs standing guard so I was not overly concerned although I still felt ill at ease. These feelings were enhanced by the fact that in order to freshen up before lying down for the evening I would have to use the bathroom facilities at the opposite end of the hotel, the bathroom next to room 109. The bathroom was over one hundred feet from the security of the dining room and I could not find the courage to take my flashlight and walk down the old corridor of the right wing.

Dennis offered to accompany me and wait while I washed and prepared for bed, but remembering the terror that I had previously experienced in the right wing, I decided that cleanliness was not next to Godliness, at least until morning.

After turning off the lights in the lobby Dennis retired to his makeshift bed in search of some well deserved rest. I stretched out on my mattress pulling the covers over my head in an attempt to keep warm during the night.

I could not sleep. Here in this huge vacant building that we had fought so long and hard for, I felt lonely and apprehensive. I had been very excited over the prospect of returning to Goldfield, although as usual it was not under the best circumstances, but now in the quiet of this room I was greatly concerned. Would returning to Goldfield prove to be another mistake, would I be sorry for leaving the comforts of Reno, and would I someday regret coming back? All of these thoughts crossed my mind as I silently argued with myself huddled under my blankets in the cold dining room. I was happy to be home, but I was also worried, worried about the conditions under which we returned to Goldfield, a decision to return in which we did not have a choice.

I was awake for hours, reliving the events of the past two years.

Interior of Drug Store, July 4, 1908

Chapter Twelve

Two years ago in January after giving up all hope of reclaiming our hotel, Dennis and I decided that we had to make one last attempt to recoup our property. We visited many law offices in anticipation of contesting this matter in court but the outcome of these visits was the same as before

Five months had gone by since we had lost the hotel and I was discouraged by disinterested attorneys, some of whom were adverse to listening to our story in its entirety. Other attorneys were reluctant to take our case because of the many complications.

At this time we were living in the Carson City-Gardnerville area and out of desperation I obtained the local telephone directory and began calling every listed law office.

My first question to the receptionists answering my call was. "Do you have an attorney in your office with any intestinal fortitude?"

In June I had an answer to this question. Yes, there was such a man, a lawyer in Minden, Nevada. I was elated and anxiously awaited our appointment. The day finally came when we found ourselves sitting in his office. He listened carefully and then told us he believed we had valid grounds for a lawsuit and would welcome the opportunity to help solve our legal problems. Unfortunately he could not act as our attorney as it would be a conflict of interest with the Real Estate Division of the State of Nevada.

As we had previously filed a complaint against the realtor with the Real Estate Division, he informed us he could not represent us as an associate in his office had recently left a position in this same state department.

He did however recommend another attorney and set up an appointment for an hour later. We drove immediately to

Carson City where this law office was located. This lawyer was very interested but he had also been employed at one time by the Real Estate Division and this again might prove to be a conflict of interest. By this time I was becoming depressed and when this lawyer made an appointment to see yet another attorney later in the afternoon, I told Dennis, "No more, this will be the last one. If it doesn't work out, were through."

Our appointment was for one o'clock. The sign on the door read Charles Kilpatrick, Attorney at Law. As we sat in his Carson City office we related all the details of the Goldfield Hotel transactions. He listened to us without interruption, and then asked us to return in two hours, during which time he would review all pertinent documents.

Two hours later we were back in his office. Mr. Kilpatrick then uttered the words that I had waited months to hear. Yes, we definitely had a good basis for a law suit and yes; he was willing to start litigation immediately. I tried to hold back my tears as I thanked him and I sincerely felt that a simple thank you was not enough. This man not only listened to us and believed in us but he restored my faith in the legal profession.

This meeting was the beginning of a long legal battle.

During this period of time we were also working with state officials on the complaint we had filed with the Real Estate Division. It was over a year before a hearing on these charges took place.

I was looking forward to this hearing but I was concerned about the men and women that were the members of the Board of Realtors. This Board of Realtors would preside over the hearing and determine if the realty agent had acted improperly during the Goldfield Hotel transactions. Would they listen to me? Would I have the opportunity to tell them of the transactions that I strongly felt were less than honest, or would they dismiss these allegations as many attorneys had done before.

It was the day of the hearing and I sat at the end of a large conference table facing the realty board members. The realtor was represented by his attorney but I was unaware that I was also entitled to legal counsel.

I was more than a little nervous when I realized that the eyes of all the board members were fixed upon me waiting to hear the facts of the Goldfield Hotel purchase.

The board was patient and fair giving me every opportunity to cite my grievance against the real estate broker. The broker's attorney questioned me repeatedly but I would not alter my statements because what I had told the board was the truth. The hearing went on for hours and when it was over we were led into an anteroom to await the board's decision.

We were in the anteroom for hours. The hearing had started at two o'clock in the afternoon and now it was one o'clock in the morning. Dennis and I spent these hours with the chief investigator from the Real Estate Division who tried to assure us of a positive outcome of these proceedings. Although the broker had admitted to some of his wrongdoings to the board, I was still worried. Would they really believe us? Someone had to.

Shortly after one o'clock we were summoned back to the boardroom. I resumed my place at the conference table where I was to hear the decision that the Board of Realtors had made. It was in our favor. I was so excited I could barely hear the Deputy Attorney General read aloud the list of charges against the broker. At this moment I felt pity for this man for jeopardizing his career, although his actions had cost us the loss of our building. It was hard for me to comprehend that someone had finally taken the time to hear my plea and as the realty board members filed past me I looked up to one of the men and said "Thank you for listening to me." He replied, "I heard you lady, I heard you." This time I could not contain my tears. That man, Bill Myers of Myers Realty, Reno, Nevada.

The months rolled by and our attorney was still working diligently on our case. As usual I was not in a good financial situation so when our attorney discussed a settlement being offered by the seller we decided to accept it.

Under the terms of this settlement a substantial amount

of money would be needed and in order to raise this amount we entered into a partnership with an investment group. A short time later the title to the Goldfield Hotel was duly recorded in the Esmeralda County courthouse in Dennis's name and mine. It was April 1979.

We were extremely anxious to see the hotel that was now legally ours, but we had to wait until the weekend before we could leave for Goldfield. We were not only operating a small shop in Reno at this time, but Mary Lynn was attending a school for handicapped children and we did not want to interfere with her schooling. Lisa would not be with us on this trip as she had married and was now the mother of an infant son. She was, however, a member of our new partnership and promised to join us in Goldfield at a later date.

Dennis, Mary Lynn and I left Reno early Saturday morning to see the hotel we had left years ago. Although it was only a five hour trip, it seemed that we would never reach our destination but eventually the old desert road brought us to the steps of our Goldfied Hotel.

As I parked the car in front of the old building, our friends Helen and Grant ran across the street to greet us. As our dear friends embraced us I realized how good it was to be back in this town we called home.

Moments later Dennis took his key and opened the padlock on the front door and we entered the building for the first time in two years. Instead of going to the piano to play our theme song he walked directly into the saloon.

I followed Dennis into the saloon and watched him as he stared at the bar as if he couldn't believe what he was seeing. It was straight, perfectly straight without a sign of ever having been warped.

I was not shocked by this discovery even though I realized it was virtually impossible for a bar so badly warped to return to its original shape.

But why this day? Why was it straight now?

During the past two years Dennis and I had many occasions to pass through Goldfield on our way to Las Vegas, and although we had been denied access to the building during litigation, we would always stop at the hotel and peer through the windows. On all of these occasions we found the bar to be in the same warped condition.

I then hurried into the dining room to check the wall. If the bar had straightened itself out, then what about the fake wall that divided the dining room into two sections? I had little time for these thoughts before I reached the wall and when I did I could only stand there in utter amazement. It was as smooth as it was the first day we had seen the hotel. A strange feeling came over me, a feeling that I was not alone and I said aloud as I stood in the dining room, "You did hear me, didn't you?" I was referring to the day that we had to leave the old building and I stood behind the bar and called out "Hotel, destroy yourself."

After I showed Dennis the wall he walked around the hotel shaking his head in disbelief. As he could not find any logical explanation for this phenomenon he began to feel more strongly that there were unseen presences in the building.

We spent several hours in Goldfield that day and then made a decision to return home by late afternoon instead of staying overnight as we had originally planned. It was April and it was much too cold to be in the building for any length of time so nightfall found us on the long stretch of highway that would bring us back to Reno.

Months went by during which we made several trips back to Goldfield when it concerned hotel business. Our partnership was not going well as I was determined to stay with our initial agreement as to the restoration of the hotel. I refused to sell it, lease it or turn it into a time-share project. This brought dissension into the partnership and when the investment group offered us a proposition pertaining to the hotel's restoration, we eagerly accepted it.

The group offered to loan the partnership a large sum of money to be used to start the restoration under the condition that Dennis and I would close our shop and take up residence in the hotel to oversee the project. We were to receive a salary from the partnership and have access to funds needed for heating, cleaning supplies and any necessities needed to make living in the building more comfortable. We were asked to leave for Goldfield in a week.

That week was very hectic. We vacated our house which was semi-attached to our shop, held a close-out sale on our merchandise and dismantled the equipment we were using to manufacture our product. We also sold our station wagon as we would be leasing a moving van for our trip to Goldfield and would purchase another vehicle from Grant upon our arrival.

At the end of the week we were ready to leave. Our business and personal belongings were stored in the front of our shop and we temporarily bedded down in our office for the night. We did not regret making this decision as our primary concern had always been to see the hotel restored to her original state and now we had an opportunity to do so.

Our business had been open less than a year and we had been doing quite well. We had made our majority share of the hotel payment and were able to meet our obligations. We did not have a reserve of funds as yet as the business was fairly new, but I was not upset over closing our shop knowing we would be giving up our income as the proposal that was offered to us would keep us in a stable financial situation.

We did not leave that week. Nor the next and not for many weeks afterwards. I became extremely distressed, our shop was closed but we still had to meet financial obligations, our house was re-rented and we were living in our office and every day brought news of a further delay. As a general partner I was entitled to be informed of the present situation on this proposal but negotiations were handled only by a family member and the investment group.

I finally received news that the other general partner representing the investment group would arrive at the office to finalize this transaction. After a brief stay he left the office to deposit the funds in the bank, promising to return in an hour. Now Dennis, Mary Lynn and I would be on our way to Goldfield within a few days.

That evening Lisa called and informed me the group "had changed their minds."

"Oh Dennis, what do we do now? We can't stay here and we can't go to Goldfield. What did they do this to us for?"

I knew we could't stay in Reno. Not only had our house been re-rented but plans had already been made for our shop and I was very angry.

"Dennis," I said "We have to go to Goldfield, we have no other place to go. We'll walk if we have to."

I telephoned one of the group members and told him of the position they had placed us in and also what I thought about it.

Several days later they agreed to finance our trip to Goldfield and as we had no other recourse we accepted their check that would cover the cost of the moving van and small expenditures.

This was the reason we returned to the hotel under these financial conditions and why I was lying awake in the dining room worried about our predicament. By closing our shop our income had been terminated and I would be unable to meet our next hotel payment.

I looked over at Dennis who was in a sound sleep, enjoying a respite from the troubles that plaqued him and wondered, "What's going to become of us now?"

We had a busy day ahead of us and I desperately tried to get some rest. I do not remember at what point I finally fell asleep.

It was the Spring of 1980.

Chapter Thirteen

Early the next morning I was awakened by a tapping on the dining room window. I opened my eyes and saw Grant's face looking down at me.

"Come on over," he said. "Helen's getting breakfast ready."

"Okay, Grant, we'll be right over as soon as we clean up a bit."

Dennis sat up quickly and I knew he was looking forward to some hot coffee and Helen's good cooking.

Tossing my blankets aside, I stepped onto the cold tiles of the dining room floor. "Damn!, it's cold, Dennis. Let's get ready and get over to Helen and Grant."

Helen would always fire up her old cast iron stove and the thought of her warm kitchen as compared to the icy coldness of the hotel sent me scurrying down the hall to the right wing where I could wash and change clothes.

In the daylight hours I was no longer frightened over the prospect of entering the old corridor that led to the bathroom and besides, I was in too much of a hurry to get to Helen's to give it much thought.

However, as soon as I was in the bathroom I felt differently about the situation. I sensed that I was not alone, that I was being watched not by one entity but by several. It was as if they had come to see me on my return home. I said to whatever was there, "you're still here aren't you, you're still here?"

That morning I set a record for the time it takes to wash and change one's clothing. I was still buttoning my blouse as I ran down the hallway into the lobby calling out to Dennis. He did not answer me, but knowing Dennis, I assumed the offer of hot coffee on a cold morning was too tempting to waste his time on washing before going to Helen and Grant, so I ran across the street and knocked on their door.

Helen opened the door and shouted "Shirley" and gave me a welcoming hug. I glanced over her shoulder into the kitchen and there was Dennis holding his coffee cup with his usual smug look of satisfaction on his unwashed face.

It was good to see our friends again. They had noticed the moving van parked in front of the hotel earlier that morning and Helen immediately began to prepare breakfast.

We spent hours visiting them in their warm cozy kitchen but then it was time to return to the hotel to unload the truck and tend to our dogs.

We set up our furniture in the dining room and made a combination living room and sleeping quarters in the area. After we hung pictures and added other decorative items the room was transformed into a pleasant looking apartment. As I looked around at this cheerful setting, I could not imagine that anything frightening could happen here but I was soon to be proven wrong.

The next few days were busy ones. After returning the moving van to a rental agency in Tonopah, we had to prepare the hotel for tours. It was too early for the tourist season and the hotel was still much too cold to welcome travelers but our "Open for Tours" signs always attracted some hardy tourists that wanted to see the building regardless of the cold temperature.

We also had to prepare a suite of rooms for our friend Chuck and his wife Leslie, a couple we had known in Reno. Chuck had always been interested in the Goldfield Hotel and we had made plans for him and his wife to live with us upon our return to Goldfield. He was due to arrive in three weeks and he and Leslie were going to open a small candy store in our former shop.

Within a week the hotel was open to tourists and although the traffic on the highway was sparse we found ourselves hosting several tours a day.

One afternoon I opened the door to a tall, heavy set gentleman who requested a tour. He introduced himself and explained that he was on his vacation and that he worked for the British Broadcasting system in England. As we went from room to room on every floor I related to him the history of Goldfield. He was genuinely interested in the hotel and after an hour conversation he turned to me and asked, "Is the building haunted?"

I hesitated before I answered, "Well, yes it is. I usually don't tell anyone unless they ask, but it is haunted. It's mostly downstairs in the right wing, in fact there is one room that I am very afraid of. I don't go in there, not alone anyway."

He then asked me, "Can I see it? You know I had a feeling it was haunted when I came in. We have many haunted houses in England, you know."

I couldn't refuse his request so I led him through the lobby and into the old corridor. I told him, "I'll go into the room with you but only for a minute, I can't stand being in there."

I opened the door cautiously and we stepped into the deathly stillness of room 109. Immediately I felt the cold chills, and the urgency to leave that I had encountered the first time I entered the room. I stood close to this man but I made sure I was near the doorway so I could exit quickly if I had to.

He started to tremble. He said, "This is terrible. I've got cold chills running up and down my spine. I'm shaking all over."

"I know," I replied. "That's what happens to me every time I walk into this room. I don't even want to be in here now."

He was quiet for a minute and then knelt down on the floor.

"What's that, what's that noise?"

I couldn't answer his question as I had never heard that sound before. It was a tapping, a loud continuous tapping coming from the crawl space area of the basement. All of the rooms in the right wing had an opening at the base of a wall that led into this section of the basement. These openings were covered by small doors and were to be used if heating and water pipes were in need of repair and were only large enough to crawl through.

He put his ear close to the lower part of the wall as the tapping continued. It was definitely coming from the basement.

He turned to me, "Is anyone in the basement?"

"No," I answered. "Dennis is in the dining room. This part of the basement is only about two feet high and the only way to get under the floors is to go through the little doors and crawl on your hands and knees."

He stood up and I saw that he was still trembling. His voice wavered as he spoke, "I've got to get out of here, this is terrible, I don't know what's in here but I've got to get out."

We hurried out the doorway and after slamming the door behind us, we ran into the lobby. I was shivering so badly I could barely speak.

"See, I warned you. I don't know what it is but that room terrifies me."

He agreed and as I looked at this tall strapping gentleman who was still visibly shaken, he erased any doubts I may have had of my feelings towards room 109.

We chatted for a while but he seemed overly anxious to leave the hotel. He could leave after this experience, but I had to stay.

Chapter Fourteen

Chuck and Leslie were due to arrive by late afternoon and I was overjoyed by the news as now there would be someone else residing in the hotel besides Dennis and I.

There was a loneliness in the hotel now, a loneliness I did not feel the first time we had lived in the building. It was because Lisa and Mary Lynn were not with me.

Mary Lynn was living in Reno with Lisa so she could complete her school semester and Lisa had just settled into her new home with her husband and newborn son. Their absence left an emptiness that I could not replace.

I missed their laughter that used to echo throughout the lobby. I missed my long talks with Lisa upon our old iron bed, but most of all I missed my little companion that was always at my side.

No longer would we take our flashlights and roam the halls seeking an explanation of the unusual sounds we so frequently heard. Nor would we spend the late summer evenings on the old pillared porch, sitting there for hours while Goldfield slept, hearing only the howl of the coyotes or the occasional barking of a dog. We would never again do any of the things that had made the Goldfield Hotel seem like home and so I was anxiously awaiting the arrival of Chuck and Leslie, hoping that their presence would help fill the void.

By early evening our friends had arrived and had selected a three room suite on the second floor. Leslie was apprehensive about staying in the hotel and Chuck would have to accompany her whenever she used the bathroom facilities in the right wing.

Within two weeks Chuck had stocked his shop and was open for business. Leslie had decided to make new living quarters in the rear of the store as she did not feel comfortable living in the hotel. Chuck was well aware of the spirits that inhibited the building as we had related all of our experiences to him when we all lived in Reno. It was quite upsetting to Leslie and she felt more secure living in the back of the shop. The only entrance to the shop was directly from the street and as it did not have an additional entry into the hotel, it was separated from the rest of the building. We shared a common wall with our side being at the far end of the dining room and if we wanted to contact each other without leaving our quarters we would just knock on the wall that separated us. There was also a hole in the wall that had been made when an electrical cable had been removed and if we needed to get a fast message to Chuck or Leslie we would knock on the wall and speak to them through the opening. We would often use this method of communication to let them know that dinner was ready to be served.

They had been in Goldfield for several weeks and it had become our custom to share dinner and spend a few hours together. Afterwards Chuck would escort Leslie to the right wing where they would use the bathroom facilities before retiring to their rooms in the shop.

On one particular night they had left early and Dennis and I were sitting in the dining room quarters reading some material on Goldfield. It was a quiet, uneventful evening and I was totally unprepared for what was about to happen.

Heavy footsteps began pounding on the floor above us as if someone was running. Dennis jumped up. "What the hell is that," he asked?

I thought about this for a moment and then answered, "Oh Dennis, we must have forgotten to lock the front door and now someone is upstairs again. What are they doing running through all the rooms, besides, it's completely dark up there?"

As it sounded as though there were several people upstairs, I told Dennis to knock on the wall for Chuck. "No, Dennis, go to his front door and get him, I'll wait in the lobby in case they come downstairs and try to leave the hotel."

Minutes later Dennis returned with Chuck and Leslie and as they joined me in the lobby we explained to them what was happening.

We decided to go upstairs and confront the intruders but leaving Leslie in the lobby as she was extremely frightened. We took Bruno, our trained watchdog, and started up the first set of steps that would lead us to the second floor. I was in a rage at this time as I was tired of people entering the hotel uninvited and unexpectedly finding them on every floor of the building including our personal living quarters. I stormed up the stairs to the first landing intent upon having a confrontation with these uninvited guests.

As I reached the landing I stopped suddenly and made no attempt to take the other steps that would bring me to the second floor corridor.

I screamed at Dennis and Chuck—"Don't go up there, don't go! Go downstairs! You can't go up because there's no one there,"

I was frightened for all of us because at that moment I realized who was running through the rooms. I also knew that if we looked in all fifty rooms on that floor that we would not find a living soul.

Dennis and Chuck retreated down the stairs into the lobby.

"Dennis, get Bruno. If someone is up there he'll find them."

Dennis sent Bruno to the second floor and we could hear the soft patter of his paws as he strolled through the hallway above.

I said to Chuck, "See, you can hear footsteps down hear, even Bruno's but the ones we heard were loud and were running.

We all stood in the lobby for a short time listening to Bruno's footsteps as he went from room to room. Satisfied that there was no one upstairs Bruno returned to the lobby. If anyone had been there this dog would have found them. He considered the hotel his territory and guarded it zealously. He was also trained to do this as I usually took him with me as I checked out the upper floors where I would encounter uninvited tourists. Bruno would run through the maze of the hotel suites and would alert us to intruders by a loud resounding bark. But this time he was silent.

Leslie was standing in the lobby visibly upset over this latest episode so Chuck thought it best to return to their shop. Dennis and I adjourned to our living quarters in the dining room to discuss the matter further.

"Dennis." I said, he was running, it's as though he wants me to hurry as if I have to do something quickly, but what does he want me to do?"

I did not get much sleep that night. I had opened the dining room doors that led into the saloon and had positioned my bed so that I could look through the saloon into the lobby. If someone did come down the stairs I would be able to see them. I also had Bruno by my side and he would not let anyone pass through the lobby unnoticed. I laid there for hours staring up at the ceiling calling out to whatever was up there. "What do you want of me, what do you want me to do? What are you trying to tell me?"

Chapter Fifteen

Warm gentle breezes replaced the cold gusty winds that had prevailed upon Goldfield during its winter season. Early spring not only brought a change of climate but also lined the highway with tourists, many of whom were anxious to see the hotel.

The lobby once again echoed the sound of Dennis's piano playing as we welcomed each tourist into our historical old building. Our days were busy ones as we proudly showed the interior of the Goldfield Hotel to anyone who requested a tour.

Evenings were spent with our friends Helen and Grant or with Chuck and Leslie and the hollowness I felt at first was beginning to subside. I could not, however, erase the fact that our partnership was not going well and that a payment had to be made on the property. We would be unable to meet this obligation due to the closing of our shop in Reno.

I also could not forget that I was sharing the hotel with spirits from the past and their lingering presence was beginning to unnerve me. It became increasingly difficult for me to enter the right wing unless I was showing tourists this particular area.

One day I thought I had found the perfect solution to entering this wing alone. I would have Bruno accompany me and wait in the hallway until I was ready to leave this section of the hotel. Bruno was very reluctant to enter the old corridor and would whimper and whine when I forced him to sit outside the doorways. If I did not call out to him constantly he would hasten back into the lobby leaving me alone. I struggled with his rebellion against staying in the corridor, but after several days I came to the conclusion it was not worth the effort. His actions only intensified my feelings towards the right wing.

Occasionally I would hear footsteps and unusual sounds

coming from the other rooms in the hotel and I was always intimidated by their presence. When I was overcome by these feelings I would leave the hotel and visit Helen where I felt a sense of security. Helen would listen patiently to my stories of these eerie occurrences and was also deeply concerned about the business aspect of our partnership. Not having telephone service of our own, all partnership calls were made through Helen and she was very much aware of the numerous offers and proposals made to Dennis and I, which as usual, never materialized.

Helen was a great comfort to me as I was utterly disgusted with the hotel transactions and of partnership business being discussed without my knowledge, when in fact, I was a general partner and Dennis and I held majority interest. It was during these times that I felt hopelessly trapped in the hotel, and deeply resented having been placed in this situation.

Our only income was from tour donations and as our car was sold in Reno, we did not have the opportunity to leave Goldfield to raise funds or interest investors. I was under extreme pressure at this time and having ghosts rattling around the building only added additional stress.

Still, my first priority was the Goldfield Hotel of which I was fiercely protective of and I felt that I had to care for it as if it were a child. But why did we keep struggling? What strange power held us to this hotel no matter how adverse conditions became?

There were also happy times in the hotel and we greatly enjoyed giving tours and as was our custom, relating Goldfield's past. I was always in a cheerful mood when we entertained guests and I would temporarily forget our problems until one day I opened the front door to play host to a mystery.

It was late afternoon when I noticed a group of what I thought were tourists standing on our front porch. As I welcomed them into the lobby I recognized one woman I had previously met before. She was a female minister and the group consisted of some of her church members. She had a mining claim in the area and she and her followers were visiting Goldfield. Her decision to call on me was based on knowledge of the hotel being haunted. I had never discussed the spirits in the hotel with any of the townspeople so I was at a loss as to how she acquired this information.

As she stepped into the lobby she said, Shirley, we're here to rid the hotel of the ghosts."

"No," I replied. "Leave them alone. I'm not into this kind of thing and I don't want to start anything. Just leave them alone."

She insisted that we go into the room that kept me in fear and force them to leave.

I explained to her I did not want to get involved in any ghost chasing and seeing that they had never hurt us I would prefer they be left alone. I was also afraid that something even stranger may occur if they attempted an exorcism. I insisted that I did not want to become involved in a ritual of any sort.

She finally asked if I would be willing to go into the room with her group and concentrate to see if I could get any strong feelings or vibrations.

Knowing that they would not leave unless I consented to doing this I relunctantly agreed. As we walked into room 109 she suggested we all hold hands in a circle, but all I wanted to do at the time was leave the room and the group. I forced myself to stay, hoping it would be over in a few minutes and they would leave. The minister closed the door of 109 and I joined hands in a circle, all the time feeling every inch of a fool.

When they asked me to close my eyes and concentrate, I did, but I did not expect to feel anything more than the usual fear. I am perceptive and I really tried to concentrate and I kept saying to myself, who are you and what do you want? I immediately sensed there was an entity in the room so I opened my eyes and looked towards the outer wall. There was a girl. A young girl, tall and slender with dishwater blond hair. Her arms were upraised as if she was trying to get out. She stood against the wall reaching upwards, a window to her left and the side wall to her right. She was clad in a bluish-green dress reminiscent of a paisley print.

"My God," I screamed, "It's a girl, she's trying to get out, she's being held against her will."

"White slavery," the minister shouted.

"No, I told her, "Not in this hotel, they didn't need white slavery, there were fifty-three cat houses in Goldfield. This was an elegant hotel, they wouldn't do this here."

I ran from the room into the lobby, shocked by this experience, my body shaking from what I had seen. These things happen to other people, not to me. But I had definitely seen that girl and I knew she was held unwillingly in that room.

The minister and her group decided to leave when they saw how distraught I had become and immediately after their departure I went in search of Dennis.

I found him in the saloon.

"Dennis," I shouted. "I saw a girl in that room," and then I frantically related to him all the details of what I had seen.

"She was standing in the center of the room, Dennis, as if she was trying to get out. Why wasn't she by the window? This question puzzled me but eventually I was to find out the answer.

Unlike all other windows in the hotel that faced the outdoors, the windows in 109 opened into a back office behind the registry desk in the lobby. A chute-like concrete slab attached to the window allowed light to enter the room but also insured privacy from the back office. Room 109 also had the adjoining bathroom so it would be a perfect arrangement if the intention was to keep someone locked inside the hotel.

I tried to calm myself after discussing it with Dennis, but I could not resign myself to the fact that I had actually seen a girl in that room. Who was this girl? What had happened to her in that room years before and why did I still feel the same terror that I felt the first day I walked into 109?

These questions were to haunt me for months. But I did not know at that time how close I was to the answer.

Chapter Sixteen

Chuck walked into the hotel one early morning and announced that he and Leslie were taking a trip to Reno to purchase additional stock for their shop and would be gone for two days. He generously offered his services and asked if there was anything he could do for me while he was in Reno.

I eagerly accepted his offer as there was some material I needed from the Historical Society. Dennis and I had previously spent a great amount of time at the Historical Society doing research on Goldfield's past and on one such occasion we engaged in a long conversation with one of the men in charge of the society. During this conversation he mentioned that as the owners of the hotel we may be interested in seeing certain photographs and legal documents concerning the Goldfield Hotel.

He related to us how his curiousity had become aroused when he was looking through boxes of donated historical papers and found photographs of buildings situated on the streets surrounding the hotel. They were not pictures of people with the structures in the background, just of the buildings themselves.

After much research he concluded they belonged in a folder containing the transcript of a Federal lawsuit involving a mining claim and dating back to 1906. I thumbed through the folder briefly but as we had been there for hours and were long overdue at our shop we decided to have copies made of this material at a later date. For over a year I had temporarily forgotten about this discussion but since the night I heard the running footsteps, I felt a nagging pressure to obtain copies of these documents.

Did the lawsuit have anything to do with the boarded up space on the basement floor? Could the boards be covering up an entrance into a mine? Would these papers give me a clue as to the identity of the spirit that walked above the dining room? I took advantage of Chuck's offer and asked him to meet with this man on our behalf and request copies of these documents.

Nothing out of the ordinary occurred when Chuck and Leslie were in Reno. We had our usual tours during the day and spent our evenings with Helen and Grant. The only deviation from our normal routine was the work we were doing on a wall. We had decided to tear down the fake wall that had divided the dining room into two sections since 1917 when Goldfield suffered a population decline.

I had great fun taking down this wall and I delighted in flinging large sheets of platerboard from my high position on a ladder to the floor below. As Dennis was working beneath me near the baseboard it became quite a challenge to attempt this feat without doing him physical harm.

Dennis was a perfectionist and he was diligently working on removing every nail that held the wallboards to the framework while I, sitting on my perch, would tear away these huge plasterboard sheets and toss them about with reckless abandon. Dennis did not appreciate my sense of humor in this situation and would give me sobering looks as I sat on my ladder in gales of laughter.

While removing the wall Dennis found a wood chisel that had been left on a cross brace and sealed inside the wall since 1917. He was elated over his find as the chisel was in perfect condition and later it became one of his prized possessions.

Dennis said it had obviously been left by a workman who must have been frustrated when he could not find it. "Dennis," I replied. "He must have really been ticked off when he remembered where he left it."

Working on this project helped ease the tension we were under and was a welcome relief from our never ending problems.

When the wall had been completely removed we sat on the wide window sills looking at the long expanse of the dining room. It was almost eighty-five feet in length and it was the first time the room had been undivided in over sixty-three years. I sat there and stared at the dining room, thinking about how beautiful it must have been when the hotel opened in 1908.

Now the only remnant of its former splendor was a pair of red velvet draperies, tattered and faded but still gracing one of the windows, a pathetic reminder of its elegant past.

The tables with their velvet chairs were gone as was the piano used for gracious entertaining, the limoge china, the engraved silverware, crystal water pitchers and vases, and everything else needed to maintain a restaurant of this era. It was all gone, stripped from the dining room years before. All that was left was this large hollow room, devoid of all furnishings, its waterstained wall and collapsing ceiling offering proof of its years of neglect.

Recalling from memory the photographs I had seen, I would envision this room as it had been at the turn of the century when it hosted its many guests from the local gold miners to the financiers of Europe, with its menu comparable to the finest dining houses in San Francisco.

It made me very sad to see the dining room in this condition and I wanted so much to restore it to its original beauty but I was financially unable to do so. At least working on the wall did help pass the time until Chuck and Leslie returned from Reno.

They were due to arrive in Goldfield before nightfall but soon it was late evening and I was becoming concerned. They would be traveling Highway 95, the major portion of which is only a two lane road with narrow shoulders leaving no room for error. Dennis and I were acustomed to driving this highway but Chuck was unfamiliar with it and had never driven on it after dark. He was also unfamiliar with the long desert stretches where cattle would loom before you without any warning and for an inexperienced desert driver this could be extremely hazardous, so I was greatly relieved when at eleven o'clock I heard Chuck's car pull up at the side entrance of the building. He had made it home safely. Seeing the lights were still on in the hotel, he came directly into our living quarters, a large manila envelope in his hand.

"Chuck," I said. "I'm so glad you made it back, we were so worried about you."

Chuck explained that they had spent more time than they had anticipated shopping for supplies, supplies that could not be purchased in Goldfield or nearby Tonopah. They had shopped extensively knowing that they would not be leaving Goldfield again for several weeks.

"But here," said Chuck as he handed me the manila envelope. "I got the copies you wanted from the Historical Society. The guy was real helpful and we stayed and talked to him for a while."

I thanked Chuck for his efforts and bid him goodnight as he and Leslie were exhausted and were anxious to retire to their bed. I was so anxious to see the documents from the Historical Society that sleep was of little concern to me.

After Chuck left, I hurriedly opened the envelope and as I pulled out the transcript a large picture tumbled out. It was an enlarged photograph of the back yard of the hotel building. A huge mound of dirt surrounding a deep hole was in the center of the yard with mining framework above the opening of this hole. On top of this high mound sat three miners looking rather dejectedly at the ground below. They

Windlass Auto Shaft on Vera claim, back of the Goldfield Hotel at the time of construction. Photo was taken on June 17, 1907, looking southwest.

were sitting at the entry of what was definitely a mine shaft, but directly behind them the photograph showed the latter stages of the construction of the Goldfield Hotel.

"Dennis, look!," I shouted. "They're mining at the same time the hotel is being built, but where is the mine, could it be in the basement?" I then took the transcript of the 1906 trial and began to read it.

After a few minutes I said to Dennis, "This is an appeal, someone lost their mine and they are bringing this suit to reclaim it."

I read the transcript of the trial for hours. I read it several times until I memorized all the facts pertinent to this case. Regardless of the evidence supporting his claim the end result was that the owner of the mine lost his appeal, the property became part of a patented townsite and the hotel was erected as planned. I sympathized with the mine owner's plight even though this incident had occurred years ago.

"It just didn't seem fair, Dennis," I said. "I don't think he should have lost this appeal, but I wasn't here in 1906 and maybe there are some facts I don't know about, but according to this transcript it just doesn't seem right to me." Over seventy years had passed since this man had lost his mine, a mine he felt was taken from him unjustly but I grieved for his loss as if it were yesterday. I wanted to reach out to him and say "I'm sorry," but it was much too late for that now. While reading these papers I found the one important piece of information that I was searching for. According to testimonies of mine owners and operators, it states that they had the ore sample assayed, ore samples taken from the main shaft of this claim located in the basement of the Goldfield Hotel.

So it was a mine. This boarded up space that intrigued our tourists and which I had been told was an outdated sump was actually an entrance into a vertical mine shaft. I had my suspicions about this space for years but now I finally knew the truth.

I called over to Dennis, "You know where that ghost walks, look up at that part of the ceiling and then look down." It was here in this small section above the dining room that the footsteps of the spirit walked above us.

Using a few calculations, Dennis determined that the space in the basement that we now knew to be a mine was directly under the area where my mysterious spirit walked.

"Oh Dennis, he was trying to tell me about the mine, he was trying to help me."

It was that night that I realized that this entity came to me in time of trouble and financial worry. As I looked back over the years I remembered that he always walked when I was deeply concerned over our position in the hotel. At that time I believed that this spirit had been the owner of the claim and was sympathetic to us because of his own loss.

It was 2:00 a.m. in the morning before we settled down to sleep but before I closed my eyes I looked upward to the area where my protector walked. "I understand what you have been trying to tell me, but what do you want me to do about this mine?"

Since that night I was never again in fear of that spirit although I was still deathly afraid of the old corridor and room 109.

The next morning after telling Chuck about the previous night's events, Dennis and I ventured into the basement to find out exactly what was under the boarded up section.

We closed the hotel to tourists so we could work uninterrupted and it took several hours to pry up and remove the outer boards. When the last board had been pulled up Dennis took the trouble light and hung it directly over the opening. It was all there, the complete framework of a mining shaft, including the ropes and bucket hoists. It was as if we had gone back into history, back into the past to the day they boarded up the old mine in 1907. We did not know what to expect when we looked down into the mine shaft but we were surprised and disappointed to find that it was filled with rocks. This situation had definitely dampened our enthusiasm over finding the mine shaft but our depression was short lived. There was but one solution, remove the rocks. As we had to host our tours during the day, we could only work in the shaft during early morning hours or in the evening. It took several weeks before each rock was painstakingly removed and at a depth of eight feet we found another boarded floor.

I begged Dennis not to stand on this floor as it could collapse and send him shooting down into the shaft below but he was determined to tear up the old floor boards. "Dennis, at least tie a rope around yourself and use this rigging the old miners set up for that purpose." At my insistence he finally consented to doing this but every minute he was on the shaft floor all I could think of was how I would get him out of the mine if he fell in.

It was a ridiculous situation. Here we were in a darkened basement, our only light coming from a small trouble lamp, with Dennis standing on the boards of an old mineshaft that had been dug in 1903. I was intrigued by all of this but I also feared for Dennis's safety.

I became very nervous and yelled at Dennis, "Get out of the mineshaft or I'll go upstairs," but I knew as I said this that I would not leave him alone. I pleaded with him to wait until we had some help but he was adamant, he was not coming up until he saw what was under the boards. I tried again, "What if the flooring breaks, you'll fall, what about those gases that form in the old shaft, the gases could kill us or blow us up."

Nothing worked. Dennis was not coming up until he looked under the boards. Eventually he loosened one of the boards and began to pry it up. Water spurted up and began to cover the shaft floor that he was standing on. He immediately pounded the board back into place but it was too late, the water was already filling the upper part of the shaft. It was not uncommon for old mining tunnels to fill with water and then recede but it would take a long time to clear the shaft.

"Well, so much for that," Dennis said. "We'll have to wait and get a pump and get that water out."

Although we were both disappointed I had at least found the solution as to why the basement floor in this section had large rocks strewn about. This was the largest room downstairs and it housed the sidewalk elevator used for deliveries, a burned out stairway leading to the kitchen, numerous shelves for storage, and was approximately two-thirds the size of the dining room. It had a four foot granite foundation wall as did the rest of the hotel but it showed no sign of damage. It always puzzled me as to why the floor was littered with those huge rocks.

Where did they come from? I had heard rumors that after the decline of Goldfield, and the hotel had very few guests, that someone involved in the hotel at that time was mining under the building. With my new found knowledge of the mine I arrived at a solution.

When the mine was shut down by the court action in 1907 the vertical shaft was filled with rocks. Whoever was attempting to mine the old claim removed all of the rocks so they could enter the drift twenty-four feet below. With the intention of re-entering the shaft but closing it off temporarily, they boarded the mine shaft at a depth of eight feet and then filled this eight feet with rocks before covering the top of the shaft The rocks that had originally filled the lower sixteen feet of the shaft were the ones still lying on the basement floor. Something prevented this person from going back into the mine, but one thing is certain. Someone was definitely in that old shaft years after it was forcibly closed.

Chapter Seventeen

Further work on the mine had to be delayed as we were summoned to Reno by members of the partnership who wished to present another proposal to us. This time they offered to withdraw from the partnership in return for a note more than several times their original investment, although the note would include the funds needed to make our late payment.

We were very hesitant about signing a note for this enormous amount of money but we were assured by a family member involved in the partnership that he would be able to raise the needed capital by selling shares of stock. On this assurance we signed the note and our partnership was supposedly dissolved.

We returned to Goldfield and told Chuck and Leslie about our latest business transaction. They were as excited as we were over the prospect of the building being restored to its original elegance and operating as a hotel as it did in 1907. We had a small celebration that night believing that at long last our financial problems had ended and our plans for the Goldfield Hotel would be realized.

My attitude during the next month had changed considerably. When I gave my tours I would enthusiastically tell my guests of our forthcoming restoration. The spirits still walked and their presence was quite obvious but it did not upset me as much as usual. I was elated over the fact that electricians would be arriving soon to install new wiring, that our roof was to be repaired and meetings were to be held pertaining to the sale of stock. At last I had found contentment living in the hotel

Dennis and I rarely left the hotel but early one evening during this time we decided to visit a local tavern and have sandwiches and soft drinks. As this was not our usual custom I neglected to turn on our lights before leaving, not

taking into consideration that it would be dark by the time
we returned.

It was a welcome change to be in the tavern that night
even though it was only a short distance from the hotel. In
small towns such as Goldfield, bars became meeting places
for all occasions and offered the only entertainment available. It proved to be relaxing listening to the music being
played on the piano and talking with several acquaintances.

One of these acquaintances was a gentle man called
Tommy. I had been told that Tommy had come to Goldfield
on the advice of an old Irishman, a man who had been a
miner in Goldfield's turn of the century boom days. In
Tommy's youth this old man had supposedly told him
numerous tales about the early days of this mining town
and would always tell him "Son, when you're older and
tired, go to Goldfield,"and years later Tommy came to
Goldfield. This is the way the story had been told to me and
I had no reason to doubt it.

When Dennis and I were ready to leave the tavern I
walked up to speak to Tommy who was standing at the end
of the bar looking out the front window. I glanced out the
window and noticed that I had forgotten to turn on the
hotel lights and that it now looked dark and foreboding.

"Look Tommy," I said as I stared at the hotel "I have to
go home to that."

"Is it haunted, Shirley?", Tommy asked?

"It's just that one room that really scares me Tommy, the
one in the right wing."

Without hesitation he answered, "I wonder if that's the
room where the girl killed herself?"

I couldn't believe what I was hearing. In fact I almost fell
off the bar stool that I had just sat down on as I had never
discussed our ghost situation with him and he was completely unaware of the spirits that roamed the building.

"What did you say, Tommy?"

Tommy looked at me and said, "Yeah, a girl killed herself, her father was supposed to have locked her up in the

room in the right wing because she was pregnant by a married man and she killed herself."

Remembering my feelings of terror in that room, I blurted out, "No, Tommy, she was murdered."

I didn't discuss the subject much longer with Tommy as I was quite shaken by this information and wanted to return to the hotel immediately. If I had known at that time what was ahead of me I would have talked to Tommy about this at great length.

As Dennis and I walked back to the hotel I said, "Did you hear what he said, I can't believe it, there actually was a girl held in that room. I never thought of a girl being locked up because she was pregnant, but that's what they would have done years ago because of the shame attached to it,"

Dennis agreed and I believe he was becoming more interested in room 109 even though he had never felt anything unusual when he had occasion to enter that room.

This new information that I had just heard about the girl in the room shocked me. Although this entity had appeared to me several months earlier, it was greatly disturbing to hear someone other than myself tell a story supporting what I had seen.

My thoughts on the girl being held against her will was that she was mentally retarded. Seeing that my daughter Mary Lynn had been born retarded, I was very much aware of the changes in care for the handicapped since the early part of the century. It was not uncommon during that era to keep a retarded person under lock and key away from family and outsiders. I was so certain that it was a mental problem that I never thought of the girl being pregnant, which was a valid reason during those years to hide someone away.

But why would the spirit of a young girl in her dilemma terrify me? I was a mother and a grandmother, I would have compassion for this poor soul, so why did I fear her?

Somehow I had to find out the truth. If the story that the old Irishman had told Tommy was factual, would understanding this erase the terror I felt when I was in room 109?

I was about to arrive at an answer to my own question. Leaving the lobby I walked through the dimly lit corridor until I reached 109. Gathering up my courage I slowly turned the doorknob and pushed the door open. As I stepped into the darkened room I called out "It's alright, I'm here to help you, don't be afraid."

I stood there motionless, my feet rooted firmly to the floor expecting a feeling of calmness, but I was gravely disappointed. The usual wave of terror swept over me in seconds. I began shaking uncontrollably and I was afraid to move, too afraid to leave the room.

But I sensed something else, something more powerful. I felt as though someone had been waiting for me to enter this room, as if I had been lured into a trap and now in their clutches. I also had a strange feeling that something was laughing sardonically about me.

Somehow I found the strength to leave the room and I hurriedly ran into a well lighted section of the hotel.

My emotions then changed from fear to anger.

What was the mystery of this room and what strange secrets did it hold?

Chapter Eighteen

The bus pulled up to the curb next to the side entrance of the hotel. It was 4:20 a.m. and the streets of Goldfield were deserted, but I knew Dennis had left the dining room entry unlocked so that I could enter the building quickly.

As I opened the door and stepped into our living quarters I heard him stir from his sleep. I knew he would ask me about my trip and I dreaded telling him the latest news.

I had left for Reno the day before for an urgent appointment with my physician. Although I had serious medical problems I was in good spirits and spent the hours on the bus daydreaming about our coming restoration. Now that our former partnership was over I was looking forward to our forming a corporation and selling shares of stock as we had been promised upon the dissolution of our partnership.

Now I would have to tell Dennis that there wasn't going to be any corporation and that we were not going to be selling any stock.

While in Reno I had been handed an envelope giving Dennis and I an ultimatum. Although we still owned two thirds of the property we were informed that in order to pursue the corporation plans we would have to sign a "power of attorney" and surrender complete control of the hotel operation. If we did not agree to this then all plans to sell shares of stock would be withdrawn.

"Dennis," I explained, "We can't do this, we just can't sign away complete control, we have others to consider like that old man that talked to us for hours while he was on a tour." This elderly gentleman had approached me about investing his life savings into the hotel. I hadn't asked him, he said he wanted to be part of the project and that he was impressed by our honesty and our plans for the building and was willing to give us everything he had. There were others who wanted to invest, trusting people who could only afford small amounts. I had to protect these people and their investments and I could not do this if I gave up complete control. Besides Dennis and I did not struggle the past years to gain title just to turn the hotel's operation over to someone else.

I was perfectly capable of managing our own hotel and realizing a profit for our shareholders. We had made a success of our previous businesses and years before I had owned and operated my own motel and I had never had a vacancy. Many times my units were filled because of former guests returning for additional visits, some staying as long as two weeks during vacation time. Many people not only returned to my motel in the Santa Cruz mountain area but recommended me to friends and relatives. I had a good business because I catered to my guests and treated them to the respect they deserved, but most of all I did everything I could to make them feel welcome and let them know I appreciated that they chose to stay at my motel.

I wanted to do the same at the Goldfield Hotel, every guest would be special and made to feel that way. I had thousands of names in our registry book that tourists had signed while taking our tours. These were the names of people from all over the United States and Europe who wanted to return to Goldfield when the hotel was re-opened. I had promised these people the services that I would extend to everyone and assured them we would keep the hotel in its original state during repairs and would not convert the building into a Las Vegas or Reno type hotel casino. Gaming would be reminiscent of Goldfield's earlier days. And I could not perceive the idea of a hired cold, impersonal money grubbing corporate manager standing behind the desk of the Goldfield Hotel, a manager that could see only dollar signs when guests entered the lobby. I knew from experience that you can successfully operate a business and still cater to your guests treating them like the valued customers that they are.

I was also chastised for wanting to hire the elderly and I adamantly stood my ground on that issue. Who was it that manned the work force in this country before parts of our society decided they were "too old?" Yes, I would hire the elderly, or the handicapped, or anyone else that was capable, dependable and needed employment. No, I would not turn over control of our hotel because I was thought of as being incapable because of my ideas. So I refused and all corporation plans were withdrawn.

Dennis was very angry but he said, "Calm down, try to sleep and we'll talk about this in the morning."

"Why? Is it going to be any better in the morning? I'm getting tired of being taken advantage of because we trust people. What's wrong with us, are we walking around with a big sign that says 'Stupid' on our chests?"

Although he was very upset Dennis said, "Sit down for a minute and I'll tell you what happened while you were gone."

He began telling his story of what had happened the previous day. "My sister-in-law Jan came into the hotel with two of her friends. She was on the way to a horse show with her Arabians and these two women were driving with her. I gave them a tour of the main floor and when we were mid-way through the rooms upstairs one of the women asked me if we lived here all alone and I told her yes, there was just the two of us and then, naturally, her next question was if the building was haunted."

"I told her to come downstairs with me into the right wing and see for herself. As we all walked through the hall we were talking about things in general, not about any ghosts. When we reached the far end of the hallway I asked all of them if they felt anything different or unusual. The woman that was curious about the hotel being haunted said that as soon as she turned the corner into the hallway she had a strange sensation of coldness, although she admitted her feelings were stronger at the beginning of the hall more so than at the end.

As we started walking back toward the lobby she suddenly stopped in front of 109. Although the door was closed she insisted her feelings were stronger by this room. She wanted to see inside and as soon as I opened the door for her she momentarily shuddered. While we were standing there I asked her what her feelings were about the room. She said she felt there was a young girl locked in this room and when I pressed her for details she said, 'I think she died in here.' She was so upset over it that she asked me to take her back into the lobby."

"Oh great," I said after Dennis finished. I just had a bombshell dropped in my lap and the first thing I hear about is the ghosts.

It did concern me though, as Dennis' sister-in-law had never seen the hotel until that day and as we did not keep in close contact she was totally unaware of anything unusual happening in the building. Dennis could barely contain himself when he was telling me about it as this was the first time he was personally involved in anything to do with 109 Although he was always informed about my experiences in the room, this was something that took place when he was there and it left him completely bewildered.

We had to end our discussion about this latest event because by now it was five o'clock in the morning and I had to get up early for tours.

The next few weeks were not easy ones. We would give our tours and smile for our tourists trying to hide the turmoil that once again had invaded our lives. But the tourist season was now coming to an end and in our spare time Dennis and I would work on the mine shaft trying to remove the water. No matter how much water we would pump or bail out it would always return to its original level by the next morning. We would just have to wait until it receded by itself, back to its underground source.

I had made arrangements to visit the Bureau of Land Management in Reno to try to obtain the mineral rights to the mine in our basement. Although I realized the chances were slight of two inexperienced people extracting ore from the old mine shaft, I was willing to try in order to save the hotel. I took the late evening bus and arrived in Reno early the next morning.

I spent over four hours at the B.L.M. office speaking with several of their agents. Each agent would call in another agent as my request seemed to be confusing to them. Finding it was an unusual and complicated situation, they were unable at first to determine if I was entitled to the mineral rights so they continued to research their maps and scan their computers. They were about to concede that these rights should go with the property until they asked me if there were any structures upon it.

I reluctantly told them that there was one building, namely the Goldfield Hotel. They left to recheck their maps and computers and returned with their final decision. "It's part of a patented townsite and you can't have any mineral rights." The agent in charge then looked down at me and jokingly asked, "What are you going to do now lady, stake a claim under Harrah's?"

I arrived in Goldfield the next morning and told Dennis my career as a hard rock miner was over before it started.

"But not really, Dennis. The agent gave me permission to go down one hundred feet to look for rocks and old relics, and if the rocks have gold in them it's not my problem. Besides, the shaft is only ninety feet deep."

Although I was terrified at the thought of going down into a vertical mine shaft I was determined to do so in order to save the hotel. Not knowing anything about mining I would revert to a woman's way of doing things by using our usual paring knife and screwdriver.

I had full intentions of extracting ore from the drift sixteen feet below, a drift fully described in the 1906 lawsuit transcript and taking just enough to satisfy the hotel obligations. Unfortunately, the shaft was still filled with water.

Years later I thought about our futile attempt to mine this old claim. We were going to try out of sheer desperation, but what might have befallen Dennis and I if we had succeeded in entering a seventy seven year old mine shaft?

Chapter Nineteen

It was Christmas and I was sitting on my bed in the old office feeling very sorry for myself. We had moved our living quarters back into the old office and adjoining bedroom because of the extreme cold in the building. These were the same quarters we had originally used when we first moved into the hotel, the rooms situated at the entry of the right wing. We only had one small electric heater and although it did not warm these rooms it did take away some of the chill.

It was impossible to live in the dining area any longer and as the heater would be of little use in a room that was eighty-five feet long, we made the decision to move back to our former quarters. We tacked heavy draperies to the two outer doors and filled in the cracks underneath them to ward off the cold winds. One small table held my hot plate and electric fry pan so I could do my cooking in the same area.

Everything we needed for housekeeping was confined to these two rooms and except for an occasional tour we seldom entered the main section of the hotel. It was much more confortable living in this small area during the winter months but it was also very frightening.

Beyond my inner door was the old corridor and room 109. We had to use the bathroom facilities, but I still dreaded walking the short distance down the hallway to reach them. I had to force myself to use the bathroom as the spirits were always there. I could sense them staring at me and hovering around until I wanted to run screaming out of the hotel. I found myself shouting at them, "Leave me alone, for God's sake, leave me alone!"

The situation was aggravated by the fact that Dennis and I were now the only ones living in the building. Chuck and Leslie had left months before. Chuck had not been doing well in his business and Leslie expressed a wish to return to college. I missed them very much after they left.

So it was just Dennis and I in this huge four story building with its one hundred and sixty-five guest rooms, living in one small corner of the main floor. Tourism was down to a few tours a week and we were very low on funds. We could not afford to buy each other a gift for Christmas, let alone celebrate. I sat on my bed that Christmas eve thinking of my children all snug in their warm homes while I was here in this cold room without any visible signs of the holiday. I thought of past Christmases when they were children, watching their faces light up as they opened their presents. I sat there for hours reminiscing about the past years when I spent Christmas in my comfortable home with a brightly lit tree surrounded by my family. The more Christmases I remembered the more depressed I became and I felt that everyone had forgotten about me. And then it suddenly occurred to me how lucky I actually was. I had all those beautiful memories and the true meaning of Christmas was not celebrations and gifts and we had much to be thankful for. I scolded myself, instead of wallowing in self pity, why didn't I get up and do something for Christmas.

We had our friends Helen and Grant directly across the street and they were expecting to share the holiday with us.

Shortly afterward I heard someone knock on my door and I was greatly surprised to see my son Steven on my doorstep. I was so happy to see him and I hoped he would be able to stay for awhile, but he and his girlfriend were on their way to Las Vegas. He told me they would be in Las Vegas for two or three days but promised me they would stay with us when they returned to Goldfield.

We spent that Christmas with Helen and Grant and it was a Christmas that I will always treasure.

Steven was back in Goldfield after several days and he and his girlfriend moved into our small quarters. It was good to have them in the hotel with us and it was no longer lonely. Steven, unlike my other children, did not have a home of his own and was currently unemployed so we welcomed him to share what we had.

Our small supply of groceries eventually began to dwindle and as our cash on hand was very low we had to take drastic measures to earn some money. Dennis and Steven unearthed some old wire cable that was half buried in the back yard. Steven said we could sell the copper wire if we could strip off the outer coating. I had never done anything like this before but I was ready to try.

It took Steven, Dennis and I weeks to strip the cable and when we finished our hands were covered with cuts and scratches. It was definitely not the type of job that one would make a career of, but it was worth the effort as it helped replenish our cash supply.

Steven decided to use his half to finance his search for employment in a nearby town. He and his girlfriend stayed with us for several weeks but then found an apartment in Tonopah as the cold and our primitive living conditions were not what they were accustomed to. Dennis and I were not living this way by choice, we just did not have any alternative.

The hotel seemed empty again after Steven and his girlfriend left but we still had our friends Helen and Grant. But this too was to come to an end. Several weeks after Christmas Helen informed us they were selling their property and moving to their home in Arizona. We had met Helen and Grant five years ago when they first came to Goldfield and we were more like a family than friends.

One of my most cherished memories of Helen and Grant was a Thanksgiving we shared with them.

We had come to Goldfield from Reno by bus, our suitcase bulging with an uncooked turkey and all of the trimmings. We had arrived about four o'clock in the morning and Dennis and I had planned to wait in the hotel until daylight. As we stepped off the bus into the cold air we saw the light in Helen's kitchen window and before we reached the hotel steps she opened the door and called to us to come in.

The warmth of her kitchen was a welcome sight. Helen had a roaring fire in her old cast iron stove and fresh coffee was brewing on top of one of its antique burners. Grant was sitting in his familiar wicker chair enjoying the heat from the nearby stove. It was a scene we had witnessed so many times before and I truly felt at home. They laughed about us carrying this huge turkey in our suitcase and then Helen said, "Hurry and stuff that turkey, Shirley, so we can get that dang thing in the oven."

We talked incessantly as we prepared the stuffing while Dennis and Grant, coffee cups in hand, were involved in their own conversation. We talked all day and through dinner when we served the turkey browned to perfection in their turn of the century oven.

I did not want that day to end for it meant leaving Goldfield but most of all it meant leaving Helen and Grant. When the time came to board the bus that would take us back to Reno, they begged us to "hurry back and move into the hotel because we miss you."

We were now back in the hotel but they would soon be gone. During the next month Grant made several trips to Arizona bringing truckloads of antiques and personal belongings to his home in Quartzsite. We would watch over Helen when he was gone as he was concerned about leaving her alone since these trips would take several days.

It was a sad day for us when the last truck was loaded and we had to say goodbye to our friends. They had asked us to join them in Arizona but we had to stay in the hotel until the legal matters were settled.

If I had known what was ahead of us the next two months I believe I would have reconsidered their offer.

Old Station on U.S. 95

Chapter Twenty

"Dennis please, take me away from here."

Even as I spoke those words I knew my plea was impossible. We had no car, no money, we had nothing.

I was too weak to give any more tours and I would spend the majority of the day under my blankets trying to stay warm. Dennis also spent most of his time under the covers as it was much too cold to function properly or attempt any projects.

I would look at him as he eagerly gave an occasional tour, his body thinned and his face looking gaunt from lack of food. Wearing his jacket that had become tattered and worn he still proudly showed his Goldfield Hotel to the few tourists that knocked on our door.

The tourists would walk away from the hotel never knowing how much their donations meant to us. We would use this small amount of money to feed our animals and use what was left for food for ourselves.

One day I felt like Old Mother Hubbard as I prepared to feed our dogs. I had nothing in the cabinet but a bag of flour. I mixed the flour with water and dropped spoonsful into boiling water. As I fed them these make-shift dumplings I said, "Sorry doggies, that's all there is." I did not know what I would feed them the next day as our cupboard was extremely bare and I also worried because there was nothing to put on the table for Dennis.

It was Dennis' daily routine to check our box at the post office and I watched him this day from the dining room windows as he walked down the street to see if we had any mail. We had moved our quarters back into a small section of this room as it was too depressing in the rooms off the right wing. It was much colder in the dining room but at least we were surrounded by windows and could see some semblance of life around us.

I remember one morning when it was very cold and Dennis called to me, "Hey look, look at the icicles on the windows."

"Oh Dennis," I answered him as I peeked out from under my covers. "I've seen icicles before."

"Oh yeah, well these are on the inside."

I looked up and there they were, long icicles hanging from the dining room windows.

I had to laugh about it, what else could I do in a situation like this?

"Don't worry about it Dennis, we're doing fine, we're freezing, we don't have any food and we're being foreclosed on because we couldn't make our payment. So what's a few icicles?"

Dennis just looked at me and said, "How in the hell did we get into this position?"

"Well Dennis, it wasn't real easy, it took a lot of 'nice' people to get us here."

As I stood staring out the window waiting for Dennis to return from the post office I thought back on the last two months. Those months had to be the worst ones that we had ever spent in the hotel.

We had tried several ways of earning money when winter had set in. Dennis had made a few dog houses out of the wood we had brought from our shop and sold them locally. We held a rummage sale on the steps of the hotel selling leftover retail stock from our store in Reno. We also sold personal items and our old books. When tourists did come into the building we would have our private collection of small historical items up for sale.

We did not have any transportation in which to seek employment in a larger town, so we had to make due with what was available to us in the hotel. We were making very little money on tour donations as we were fortunate to have two or three tours a week.

As it became increasingly colder in the building minor chores like cooking meals and cleaning the lobby became very difficult as we were living in an average temperature of ten to twenty degrees. It was always much colder in the hotel than it was outdoors because of its high ceilings, two foot thick walls and marble tiled floors. On sunny days the temperature outside would rise but the hotel remained the same.

Taking a daily bath in the building was a treat only for polar bears. Bathing in cold water and stepping out into frigid temperatures was less than pleasant. It was during these months that I set a record for bathing quickly.

We were unable to do anything that required great physical exertion but at times we had to be active to fight off the cold. As the weeks went by our money supply became dangerously low and we grew hungrier each day. I did not know how much more we could endure but I was soon to find out.

My tiger striped cat became suddenly ill and I laid him on the foot of my bed, the electric heater positioned on a chair directly behind him. I was unable to take him to a veterinarian as we did not have a car or any funds available. The nearest veterinarian was almost two hundred miles away and I would have hitchhiked if they would have cared for my cat and billed me for the services.

But I had to sit by and watch him suffer. Every day I prayed that God would take him and remove his agony, but every morning when I woke up and petted him he would cry out to me in a feeble voice, he was crying to me for help. He relied on me to help him, me who had always cared for him and now there was nothing I could do and he didn't understand why.

I had always been able to take care of my animals but in our present circumstances I was helpless to do anything. I couldn't bear to see him suffer any longer but I kept him close to me and when I gently petted him he would always respond with a pathetic mew. This went on for a week and I could not bear seeing my cat in pain any longer.

I was holding his frail little body on my lap trying to comfort him when out of extreme frustration I screamed, "You bastards, how could you do this? I don't care what you did to me, but look what you did to my cat." I was cursing all of them that had contributed to our being in this deplorable situation.

Nine days later my precious kitty died and Dennis gently wrapped him in a blanket and placed him in a box. The box would have to stay in the basement to be buried later when the ground was no longer frozen.

To this day I cannot forgive them for what happened to my cat.

I didn't want to stay in the hotel after this incident as I was concerned for my other animals, but I had nowhere else to go.

We did have one ray of hope however. An investor that had come into the hotel shortly after Christmas. He spoke with Dennis at length and had expressed an interest in the building. Although Dennis had told him that time was of the essence due to the foreclosure he had Dennis call him once a week from a phone booth for further discussions and this had been going on for over two months.

My present situation was now at a critical stage, we had absolutely no money and we were completely out of food.

My thoughts were interrupted as I saw Dennis returning from the post office with an envelope in his hand and a smile on his face.

"What does he have to smile about?" I wondered as he walked through the door. He's cold, he's shabby and he doesn't have anything to eat."

"It's from Helen," he said. "This should cheer you up."

I opened the envelope anxious to read her letter and a much smaller envelope was tucked inside. It was so tiny I couldn't imagine what was in it. I almost cried when I saw what it was. It was a folded up twenty dollar bill.

Somehow, Helen always knew.

I was thankful for this gift of money that we so desperately needed and I knew we had to be cautious when buying groceries at the one small market that we had in town. I had to stretch this twenty dollar bill for food over the next week so I decided to go to the store myself.

This would be a difficult task for me as my physical problems had worsened due to the cold, stress and our current diet. During the past two weeks I was barely able to walk but I was looking forward to going outdoors and to me it was a challenge to see if I could make it.

It took me several minutes to walk across the street where the store was located as my legs were shaking with every step I took. I had to hold on to the wall of the market in order to open the door, but I had made it. I shopped prudently as grocery prices in a small desert town are much higher than in a city supermarket.

I was pleased with my purchases and in a staggering manner I returned to the hotel feeling very proud of myself for accomplishing this feat.

I was just showing Dennis what I had bought when one of the local women burst into the dining room.

"Shirley!" she shouted. "Do you know what they're saying? I was standing right there when you left and someone said, 'Look at Shirley, she's so drugged up she can hardly walk',"

I became almost hysterical upon hearing this and shouted back at her, "What do they know about anything, I hardly even take aspirins, I've got a bone and muscle disease, and I have diabetes, don't they know what it took for me to cross the street? What do they know about anything?"

After she left I sat there and cried.

What did they know of what we had been going through and how dare they say something like that?

I could not console myself by the fact that it was just a few gossips that had said it, and I did realize that there were kind and gentle people in Goldfield, but I was too hurt to think about that now.

It was after that episode that I turned to Dennis and pleaded, "Please take me away from here."

Chapter Twenty-One

"Just as I am without one plea."

I sang the words to one of our favorite hymns as Dennis haltingly played the piano with hands stiffened from the cold. It was our custom to begin each day with this song and then we would sing the "Battle Hymn." Somehow it always gave us the strength to face another day. Although I became somewhat hardened by the events of the past years I had never lost my faith. Many times I felt it was faith alone that kept me going.

Our conditions in the hotel were about the same except for one slight improvement. The weather was still bitterly cold but we were hosting a few more tours, as winter travelers, commonly known as "snowbirds", were passing through Goldfield on their way to warmer climates. Steven had injured his spine on his job in Tonopah and now he and his girlfriend were temporarily staying in the hotel.

Steven complained that it was much too cold in the building and he convinced Dennis that they should fire up the old cast iron cookstove that had been in the hotel since it opened in 1908. Dennis had moved it from the kitchen into the dining room several years before.

They made a hole in the boarded up window directly behind the stove and put the stove pipe through the opening, then attached another section of pipe to it so it would extend upward on the outside of the building. This would vent the smoke when they had a fire going in the stove. It took them days to set up the stove but they were finally ready to start the fire and they assured me we were going to have heat. I was a little wary of using this old stove but I was too cold to discourage them.

We were expecting heat but all we got was smoke. Smoke belched out of every part of that old stove until it filled the dining room. Steven and Dennis were hurriedly trying to put out the fire in the stove and fan the smoke. I grabbed a cigarette and began smoking furiously in front of the dining room window in case one of the townspeople walked by and decided to call the fire department. The hotel was never in any danger of fire, only smoke, because Dennis and Steven had neglected to find out that stove pipes had to extend higher than the building.

We were all living in the dining room and to pass the time we would talk about the ghosts that inhabited the building, never knowing that Steven was soon to be visited by the spirit that walked above.

Dennis was still in contact with the invester he had met in February and we were requested to meet him in Reno at the office of his Nevada attorney. He sent us the money for bus fare so that we could join him in Reno when he arrived from San Francisco.

Steven and his girlfriend were to stay in Goldfield and care for the hotel as we would be gone overnight.

Upon our return to Goldfield Steven's girlfriend said, "Steven, tell your mother what happened while she was gone."

"Well," he began. "I had just fallen asleep when I heard a loud noise. I sat up and then I heard heavy footsteps coming from the ceiling."

I interrupted him at this point and said "You mean up there, Steven", as I pointed to the section where the spirit always walked.

"How did you know?", Steven asked.

"Because that's where he always walks, but go on, tell me what happened then."

Steven went on with his story. "After that I went back to sleep. Three times I woke up because I heard a loud bang and each time I saw a trap door. Under the trap door was a hole but there were thin boards around the hole." He then showed me with his hands the approximate size of the trap door.

He continued on. "I wasn't dreaming this, I saw it. Three times this happened. I would hear that bang, wake up and see the trap door. It was really weird, it had those narrow boards under it but there was also a hole."

"Steven, I know this hotel better than anyone else, Dennis and I know every inch of it and there is only one trap door in the hotel like it. It fits the description perfectly, except for the little boards. I don't remember if it had any. It's the one in the old office."

Steven could not possibly have seen this trap door before. When we used this room for part of our living quarters it was not only covered by an old carpet, but a bed was standing on that section of the floor. When we moved our living quarters into the dining room we used the room for storage. Large antique trunks, a clawfoot bathtub and several other heavy items were sitting on the floor directly over the area where the trap door was located.

There wasn't any way that Steven could see the floor, let alone the trap door. There were so many additional things stored upon these larger items that I hesitated asking Dennis to remove them, but I had to find out if this was the trap door Steven had seen when he was visited by my protective ghost.

Dennis was not exactly thrilled about moving everything out of the way. The bathtub and trunks were not only heavy but he had stacked so many things on top of them in order to save space.

However, he was much too curious to refuse, so a few minutes later he and Steven were busily removing everything that covered the floor. Then they took the old rug and pushed it aside exposing the trap door.

Dennis had to pry up the sides of the cover with a screwdriver while we all stood by impatiently. When it was finally opened we immediately saw the narrow wooden slats that surrounded the opening.

"That's it," said Steven. "It has to be it, it's the same size and it has the little boards with the hole in the middle."

The narrow slats were set diagonally in each corner of the opening and it definitely was the size Steven described to me when he first told me about his experience.

"Steven, that ghost always comes to me in time of trouble. He was obviously concerned about that meeting and as I wasn't here he came to you. He's trying to tell me something, something to help me. He wants us to look in the basement."

The basement under this trap door was not much higher than a crawl space but Dennis and Steven were determined to go on a search. They crawled around that section of the basement for hours using their flashlights to guide them. Dennis said they needed more light so I dropped the trouble light down to them after adding a long extension cord.

I could hear them as they crawled under the various rooms in the right wing. Putting my apprehensions aside I walked into each room when I heard them and opened the little doors used for entry when there were plumbing problems. This way I could see them no matter where they were. It was over two hours before I heard them say "We're coming up."

"Here, take these," Dennis said to me as he started to pull himself up through the trap door into the old office. Steven followed him up and the two of them stood there covered with dirt from the basement.

"Where did you find these?" I asked as I looked at what Dennis had handed me. There were several glass milk bottles and numerous empty wadded up cigarette packages. They were Chesterfield and Lucky Strike packages and I knew they were quite old as the Lucky Strike packages were green. In World War II the company sent all green packages to service men and adopted a new white one for civilians.

Steven and Dennis were disappointed at not finding anything valuable but I told them, "No, no, you don't understand, you weren't supposed to find something you could hold in your hand. It's in the ground. It's the dirt. Remember Dennis, the stories we heard about someone trying to mine under the building years ago? It has to be true, why would all those cigarette packages be lying around? Someone had to be down there for weeks or months to accumulate all of those. It has to be the dirt he wants us to explore. Don't forget we had that soft dirt in the center of the basement assayed and it did contain a small amount of gold. When our mine owner friend looked at the dirt and the assay report, he said if we dig deeper and it got darker we would find a higher quantity of gold. Don't you see what he's trying to tell us, why he came to Steven when we were gone?"

I was still tired from our long bus trip from Reno so after we put the old office back into order I went into our living quarters to get some rest.

I could not rest too easily though as I was thinking about the upstairs ghost. Why was he concerned enough to awaken Steven? I assumed he was worried about our meeting in Reno. I, too, was concerned about the meeting. I had gone to Reno in a highly agitated state to begin with as one of the reasons the meeting was being held was that this family member had already given the investor an option to purchase the one-third of the property that he held title to. This percentage was obtained when I unwittingly signed a document as a protective measure for a close family member. Several months later when I refused to grant complete power of attorney, this paper was duly filed and recorded in June of 1980 in the Esmeralda County courthouse in Goldfield, Nevada. Two weeks later I was devastated to discover that the "indenture" we signed was actually a quit claim deed to one-third of our property. Now I felt that we would not have much choice in any agreements to be discussed and I had also recently discovered that Dennis and I were the only parties that signed the note when the partnership was dissolved and that only our majority share of the hotel and property could be foreclosed upon.

It also meant that Dennis and I were the only ones responsible for the note in the amount of one hundred and forty thousand dollars. This was the same note that I was assured would be met by the sale of stock by this same family member.

As I had not yet become immune to uncovering startling facts I was naturally very upset over these upcoming negotiations. Was the spirit that walked above me also concerned?

I was so engrossed in my thoughts that I did not hear Steven talking to me.

"Did you hear me?" he said in a loud voice.

"No, Steven, I was thinking. What did you say?"

Steven replied, "I said, why don't we have a seance and find out who that ghost is and what he wants?"

"No, Steven, no seance. I don't like them. I'm also afraid of them and I just don't get involved in that kind of thing."

Steven was persistent, "What about just a little seance? We'll put a candle on that table over there and we'll have a small seance, just the four of us."

"Steven, I told you once and I'm not going to tell you any more. I don't like seances, they scare me, and I think I already know who the ghost is, he's probably the owner of the mine. Now leave me alone and let me rest. There is no way we are holding a seance in this hotel."

***

Steven placed the candle on the small table in the dining room close to the section where the spirit walked.

He could be very convincing and would usually get his own way, especially when it came to his mother. He told me this was not going to be a seance, we were just going to sit at the table with all the lights turned off while I concentrated. Except for the burning candle we would be completely in the dark.

I finally agreed, "Okay Steven, I'll sit there and concentrate but I'm not calling on my spirits."

Dennis refused to join in. He was comfortable lying on his bed and he refuse to join us. "I'll just watch from here," he said.

The three of us sat at the table not making a sound. I closed my eyes and concentrated on the name of the mine owner, the one who appealed to the court in 1907.

I felt absolutely nothing. I sat there for a few minutes until I said, "I'm sorry Steven, I don't feel a thing. I guess it's not him so why don't we just forget about the whole thing?"

He said, "Wait, what was the name of the man you were

talking about the night all those things happened in the lobby? Remember, you told me all kinds of weird things went on?"

He was referring to the first night we had spent in the hotel, the night we slept in the writing alcove with Lisa, Jim and Sally. That was the time we heard all the noises and footsteps and I found I was unable to walk past the piano to the front door. I was very surprised that Steven remembered this as it had been at least five years since I had told him this story and he didn't seem to be very interested at the time.

"You mean Mr. G., Steven?" I had no sooner spoken those words when I felt a warmth surrounding me and a sense of activity. It was as if he was standing next to me. I was certain that this was Mr. G.

I spoke to him aloud. "It is you, isn't it? It was the first time this spirit had communicated with me and his answer was "yes". It was not really a voice I heard, more like a strong thought but I definitely knew his answer. I continued speaking to him about something I was searching for in the hotel. He told me where I could find it, in a place I had never expected it to be. Unfortunately, I would have to get through a four foot granite foundation to reach it. To this day it is my secret and it cannot be revealed unless the hotel reverts back to Dennis and I. I wished I had asked him about the girl in the room but I was still shocked by his communication with me. He had given me an answer to a question that plaqued me and I was too excited to pursue my conversation any further. Looking back to those years I regret not speaking to him often, I did not fear him, I just did not think about it.

I did often wonder why Mr. G., being such a prominent man in Goldfield's history, was trying to help me.

I got up from the table as I was anxious to check out the basement and locate the area where I might find what I was looking for. After measuring and calculating this area I conceded that Mr. G. was right. It had to be where he said it was.

Now I had to get some rest.

Steven and his girlfriend were sitting up on their bed and Dennis was lying on his. I walked over to the table to blow out the candle and put away the extra chairs, when I heard Steven call to me. "Look," he shouted. I followed the direction of his eyes and saw he was staring at my wrought iron lamp that was hanging from the ceiling in the dining room. The lamp was at least five feet in length and made in the Mediterranean style of iron grillwork. It was extremely heavy and I was not able to lift it by myself.

It was moving, slightly swaying back and forth in my direction.

"It' moving," Steven said. "Nobody bumped into it and the door is not open, but it's moving."

Even if the door had been opened it would have taken a gale whipping through the building to move that lamp.

For some reason I was not surprised to see the lamp swaying and I felt certain I knew who was doing it.

I turned around and looked at Steven, "Watch this," I said as I moved in the opposite direction. The lamp slowed to a halt and then began swaying in the direction of where I had just walked.

"See, he just wants me to know he's still here, don't worry about it."

I was amazed at how calmly I was taking this as ordinarily I would have been very frightened. Every one of us had seen it and there was no denying that it had happened, but maybe it was just too bizarre for my mind to accept it.

That night I was very close to the answer I was seeking and although I was unaware of it at the time, the mystery of the spirits would be solved in less than three months.

***

Chapter Twenty-Two

"We're damned if we do, and damned if we don't."

This is the only way I could described the position we were in when it came to making a decision about entering the partnership agreement.

It was difficult to make a decision under our circumstances. We were under threat of foreclosure. A friend in California who had a small interest in the property was actively seeking investment money and was begging us not to sign this agreement, while the family member was threatening to put us into a Bankruptcy Chapter if we didn't.

But if we didn't do something quickly we could lose the hotel altogether.

Dennis was adamantly against it and he was upset that the long drawn out conversations he had with the investor had cost us so much time that our foreclosure was almost imminent. One third of the property was already on an option to purchase so it didn't leave us too much choice in the matter.

Dennis and I had spent many hours at the conference table of the investor's attorney, reading stacks of legal agreement documents only to have changes made and re-read them again. I did not fully understand the context of these papers as the wording was in typical legal language. We needed an attorney desperately, an attorney that would look out for our best interests, but we could not afford one.

We were in a constant turmoil and under extreme pressure with time running short.

"Dennis, we can't lose our hotel, not after everything we've been through, but there's something wrong with the agreements and I don't really want to sign them. It just isn't fair." I said this to Dennis even though I knew that these were the same thoughts he had.

There were parts of the agreement that sounded benefi-
cial to us but there were others that were very hard to agree
to.

In return for giving the investor control we were assured
that the hotel would be restored in a year, we would be able
to lease back our former shop and plumbing would be
installed for a business we would be able to open. We
would stay on as agents of the hotel and would receive a
salary by our own partnership, and we were also told we
could reside in the building until the restoration was completed. There were also many negative aspects to the
agreement.

We were also given the option of a complete sale of our
interest, but this was based on the value the family member
set on his sale option which was a fraction of the hotel's
value. In fact, the entire agreement was based on this value.

At that time I wished I could just lock myself in the hotel
and shut out all of our problems. The only solace I had
found recently was in the hotel although our living conditions had not changed. We still did not earn enough money
from tours to eat properly or buy necessities, but although it
was still a struggle living in the hotel, I did not want to just
give up our property.

During these times of partnership discussions in Reno I
found it very relaxing to give tours when I was back in
Goldfield.

One Sunday afternoon I gave a tour to three young men.
They had recently moved to Tonopah and were employed
by a mining company. Being new to the area they were
driving around exploring the surrounding territory and
ended up on the steps of the Goldfield Hotel.

They were enjoying their tour so much that I took them
down into the basement and let them view the old mine
shaft and then I showed them all the rooms on the upper
floors, taking care not to miss anything. I was impressed by
their enthusiasm and for the first time in weeks I felt calm
and relaxed.

One of the young men asked, "Got any ghosts in here?"

I laughed and said, "Yes, we do, but they all live
downstairs."

He just didn't seem the type to be interested in ghosts so I was surprised by his question. I then explained to them briefly about the hallway being haunted but I did not go into any detail.

Naturally they asked to see the hallway and I couldn't refuse them as they were having a good time and I was in a good mood.

I walked them through the small hall that would lead us to the old corridor but stopped before we turned the corner.

"Stand here for a minute," I said, "and see if you feel any differently than you did upstairs."

We stood there for a few moments and then the same young man said, "There is something strange here, I can feel it."

When he said that I offered to show them Room 109.

"This is my spooky room and I'm afraid to go inside, but I'll wait by the door and you see what you think about it."

When all three of them walked into the room I felt fairly protected and decided to join them. Nothing had changed, I had my usual sensations and started shaking.

I was not aware as we were all standing in 109 that Steven's girlfriend had gone into the adjoining bathroom and closed the door behind her.

"Do you feel anything in this room?" I asked them.

The young man answered, "Yes, I do, I feel like something bad happened in here, like someone was murdered."

I was taken aback by his statement. I didn't expect this kind of answer from him and it was so reminiscent of Dennis' experience with his sister-in-law's friend.

I then said, "Gentlemen, this room bothers me, It's time to go back into the hallway and talk about it."

We left the room and stood in the corridor in front of the bathroom door. I continued on with our conversation. "Okay, you think someone was murdered, do you have any feelings about whether it was a male or female?"

"I think it's a girl, a girl with blond hair."

This remark sent cold shivers through my body and I decided to tell them about the girl I had seen in the room.

As there were other tourists in the lobby with Dennis I

thought it best if we just talked about it in the old corridor. After all, I was in the company of three hardy mining men.

I spoke quietly when I related my story to them and except for the sound of my voice the hallway was quiet and still. They were deeply engrossed in what I was saying but I could see that they were becoming rather nervous. I was about to suggest that we adjourn to the lobby when,, without any warning, the bathroom door opened. I let out a horrendous scream, and three hardy miners almost dropped to the floor.

I looked up in time to see Steven's girlfriend coming through the bathroom door, but it was too late, the damage had already been done. Four people had just been reduced to quivering wrecks. So much for my day of calm and relaxation.

However, I would have rather faced the ghosts than face the legal matters during the next few weeks.

Hours at the conference table, more documents, more changes, more discussions. This went on for days. There were postponements and delays. There were hopeful moments when the right to foreclose by an out of state title company was questioned, but this was replaced by a feeling of depression when we were told they did have the authority.

We had reason to doubt the validity of the foreclosure due to discrepancies in past agreements but we did not have any legal counsel of our own and we had no one to go to for the help we desperately needed.

The one man who could have helped me was working against me for his own benefit and our greatest pressure was lack of time.

I felt that there was something terribly wrong with the foreclosure and the agreements but I had absolutely no funds or the transportation to seek professional aid.

I was emotionally distraught at this time and after one of the final days at the conference table I was admitted to the cardiac care ward in a local Reno hospital. Although warned by the physician of the consequences of these business transactions I was given no respite from them.

Two hours after my release from the hospital I was driven to Los Angeles by someone else's request to seek an alternative solution to the partnership.

The next day was spent in another long discussion over the pending agreement but by early afternoon we were on the highway to Reno after an upsetting incident pertaining to business.

I was totally exhausted and I had to admit that after five long years I felt the pain of defeat.

On the drive back to Reno I pleaded with Dennis to sell our interest out completely. "Please take the buy-out Dennis, we can use the money to start up a business far away from Nevada and maybe someday we'll be able to forget about the hotel.

Dennis was not agreeable to the idea.

"Then what are we going to do, sign the papers? We don't have much choice. If we had some time we could work something out but we're going to be foreclosed on very soon. We don't have any money, we don't have an attorney, so what do we do?"

Dennis just grumbled but I continued on, "I'm going to tell you something, no matter what we've been told you'll never see any money out of that hotel for five or ten years but most of all you will never be part of that hotel, I can guarantee it."

My feelings were very strong on what was going to happen if we entered the partnership.

Dennis finally said, "Alright, I'll take the damn buy-out."

He then started talking seriously about it. We could make a new life somewhere else and we would have the funds to open a new business and live normally for a change. It wouldn't be easy to leave the hotel but maybe it would be for the best.

When we arrived in Reno we boarded a bus for Goldfield and upon our arrival I immediately called the investor's attorney. I told him of our decision to sell our interest and he asked me to wait by the telephone booth while he contacted the investor, who would be returning my call.

After a short wait the telephone rang and it was the investor. He informed me he couldn't go through with this transaction if Dennis and I were not involved. He went on to say that he couldn't possibly attempt this project without our experience or expertise, that he needed us in this partnership.

Was I wrong about my misgivings, could I have misjudged his intentions? At any rate we had no choice as he refused to purchase our interest.

I walked back to the hotel and said, Dennis, he says he needs us, that he can't go ahead with the project unless we're in the partnership." Dennis seemed pleased with this and said, "Well, maybe it will work out anyway."

Steven drove us back to Reno where we signed the partnership agreement for the Goldfield Hotel.

If we had known at that time that the foreclosure had been postponed to a later date and we had definite cause to stop the foreclosure due to the note being possibly invalid, we never would have signed the agreement. Several people knew this as the agreement was being notarized, but this information was intentionally withheld from us.

It was May 18th, 1981.

Chapter Twenty-Three

It was all over. Dennis and I were now in a new partnership and eagerly looking forward to the restoration of the hotel. It was May and the warmth of Goldfield crept into the building and replaced the icy coldness that had been our constant companion during the winter months.

We were now busily engaged in cleaning the hotel using supplies we had purchased before leaving Reno. I hired help to wash the large plate glass windows that abounded in the hotel while Dennis and I worked in the interior and after a few short weeks the hotel was once again ready to accept visitors.

One of our first visitors was to be the architect involved in the restoration. He and his son were to stay in the hotel with us while he made his inspections and laid out plans for this project.

There was an excitement in the hotel and as we welcomed tourists we were able to tell them that the old building would be re-opening to the public by the next year. We also did not have to worry about being hungry any longer as our financial situation had changed.

As we had not yet purchased another vehicle, Steven had driven us to Las Vegas where we bought a large supply of groceries and other needed necessities and I was now able to feed and care for my family and pets in a wholesome manner.

Most of our misgivings about our partnership had faded away and we were determined to do what was best for the hotel and with the financial changes in our lifestyle we were beginning to feel contentment after the many years of struggle.

The spirits had been unusually quiet, but it was as if they were brooding and silent. I could sense them around me but I also felt a feeling of resentment. I tried to ignore this as I did not want anything to mar our new found sense of security.

The architect was due to arrive in a few days and we were looking forward to his week long stay. I planned a menu and stocked up cold drinks for the hot summer days. I wanted everything to be perfect for the architect and his teenage son. I told Dennis that we should not discuss our ghost situation with them while they were staying in the hotel but just try to entertain them when they had free time.

I was elated the day I saw the camper truck pull up to the curb in front of the hotel steps. The architect and his son had arrived. It not only meant the beginning phase of the restoration but Dennis and I would have guests in the old building again.

As we went outside to greet them we found both father and son were congenial, outgoing people. After a few minutes conversation we felt very much at ease with them as if they were old friends.

On their first evening in Goldfield we took them to a local saloon where they enjoyed live foot-stomping western music and pizza served from the bar's kitchen. It was an enjoyable evening but after a few hours we all retired to the hotel as we all had early morning schedules.

As they had preferred to bed down in the lobby Dennis and I had set up their sleeping arrangements in a large corner near the entry to the saloon area. Although we had moved our sleeping quarters to upstairs bedrooms, I preferred sleeping in the dining room while they were staying there.

The next morning the architect began his inspection of the building. He checked the support beams, the walls and the foundation. When he told me the building was structurally sound I felt like a mother hearing of her child's good report card.

"I knew it," I told him, "she passed with flying colors. I just knew she was sound." I was so proud that this old structure had weathered over seventy years of changing climates and neglect but was still solid as a rock.

Later that evening the architect and his son joined me on the front porch. We talked of Goldfield and its historic past but then suddenly the architect interrupted me,

"Shh!" he said, "listen, What's that sound?" As he was saying this he walked to the opposite end of the porch and knelt down in front of the small windows that were just inches from the porch floor. These were basement windows that were on the upper portion of a wall in the workshop area below. I walked over to him as he laid down and put his ear close to the windows.

It was the tapping sound, the same sound I heard in 109 the day I was in that room with the gentlemen from the British Broadcasting Company.

Dennis was inside the hotel and I called to him and asked him to come outside on the slight chance that he might have been involved in some work that would cause this sound.

Dennis walked out onto the porch but the tapping continued. The architect was baffled by these strange noises and could not offer any solution for them.

I told him that the closest I could get to recognizing the sound was that it vaguely resembled the reverberation of a radiator pipe if something was knocking against it. We asked Dennis to go back into the hotel and knock against a radiator steam pipe. He did this but it did not solve anything. We could not hear anything from the steam pipe, but the tapping continued.

The architect agreed that there wasn't any logical explanation for these noises and he was mystified by this occurrence. It was then I told him of the spirits that inhabited the hotel and of the experiences that I had had with them.

We sat for hours on that old porch talking about the ghosts that lived within. It was soon time to retire for the night and as usual I found it difficult to sleep.

I thought of the tapping sound. It was definitely the same tapping I had heard in room 109.

Why had I only heard it twice, and why, on both occasions did it happen when someone was with me? Were they trying to send me a message, and if so, just what were they trying to tell me?

I hadn't expected anything unusual to happen that night
and I was slightly upset over this latest happening. Did this
mean that there were more ghostly experiences ahead of
me? I was not prepared nor willing to live with these spirits
on a daily basis and the thought of additional encounters
with them frightened me.

I tried to keep busy and ignore these unearthly presences
but it proved to be beyond my control.

After the architect and his son had left Goldfield I was
discussing these events with a local Goldfield woman.
When I told her of my dog Bruno being very frightened of
the corridor she offered to bring her dog over to see its
reaction to the hallway. She informed me that her dog was
very sensitive and would be able to sense anything unusual. She walked her dog through the small hall and then
entered the old corridor. When the dog approached the
section near 109 it bolted and ran into the lobby. She then
leashed the animal and again led her through the smaller
hall, but upon walking through the right wing the dog
strained at the leash and began pulling the woman toward
the lobby.

She then told me, "There's something down there alright. I know this dog and she's never done this before,
something is scaring her."

I wished I hadn't let her bring the dog into the hotel as it
intensified my fear of the right wing, but she was so intrigued by the mystery of the building that I consented to
her doing this.

A few days later this same neighbor asked me if we
would show the hotel to a lady whose car was being repaired in her shop and as the repair would take hours, this
lady would appreciate having something to do while she
was waiting.

I was very busy at this time so I asked Dennis to give her
a short tour of the building. Dennis showed her the lobby
and saloon area and gave her a brief tour of the upstairs.

Hours later my neighbor returned and said, "Shirley, that
woman is an Italian psychic, her car broke down while she

was traveling. Do you think I could bring her back here to see what she thinks of the room?"

As I now had free time in my schedule, I agreed. "Okay, but don't tell her about the room being haunted. Just tell her that she missed seeing part of the hotel and we'll walk her down the hallway and we won't say anything. We'll just turn her loose and see if she feels anything."

A few minutes later I was escorting this psychic from Italy through the right wing. As I approached the entry of the corridor I pointed to a door to my right and said "this used to be an old office that was rented out when the hotel first opened." I tried to appear nonchalant in my conversation as I showed her the first few rooms.

She stepped ahead of me and walked toward room 109. She peered in and stood there for a short time. She walked into the room as I stood in the hallway approximately five feet from the doorway.

I reeled backward when I heard her scream. She tore past me as she ran out of the room on her way back into the lobby screaming with every step she took.

"I'm sorry, I'm sorry, I never did this before, ask my husband, I never did this before." She continued on, "That room is evil, it's evil, they'll kill you, they'll kill your animals. Get out of this hotel, get out now, they'll kill you, they're evil."

She kept shouting these words as she flung herself against the piano in the lobby, pressing her hands on top for support.

I tried to calm her although I was shaking from the outburst. She kept insisting to me, "There is something bad in there, you've got to get out of the hotel."

She asked, "Are your animals near that room?"

"Well," I answered, "my two dogs sleep in the room behind the registry desk and that wall is next to that room."

"Get them out," she shouted again. "They will kill your dogs."

"No!" I answered her. "There is a much greater spirit than the ones in that room. I will just ask God to protect my animals. They're not going to hurt them. Besides, they have never harmed us and I hardly think that they are going to kill us."

I was amazed that I had become quite calm over this situation and I found myself trying to reassure this psychic. I had never had any fear of being in danger from these spirits and I did not believe any harm would come to my animals.

I am sure she felt evil in the room but misinterpreted her feelings to where she felt Dennis and I were in danger. She did not wish to stay in the hotel any longer and apologized many times over for her emotional outburst.

As she left the hotel she said, "I'm really sorry, this has never happened to me before, but there is something terrible in that room and I've got to get out of here, but leave, please leave this hotel."

I was not frightened by this episode and I had no intention of running out of the hotel, but I was beginning to grow weary of all of these eerie events.

Although our living conditions had improved the ghost situation had not. I realized that this was not a normal way of life and I did not know how much longer I could endure sharing a home with these entities.

I was becoming increasingly wary about whether or not I could actually leave the hotel. It was such a strong feeling that I felt intimidated by it. I was almost afraid of what might happen if I did try to leave permanently, and if they would really let me go. I didn't tell Dennis about these thoughts as after our long struggle for the property, I didn't feel that he would understand my apprehension about living in the hotel.

But every day I felt the spirits coming closer and closer to me.

Chapter Twenty-Four

"Dennis, they're going to do a television show about the hotel." I had just returned from a business shopping trip from Reno with this latest news.

As the plumbing that had been promised to us had never been installed in our shop we were unable to open our proposed delicatessen as we had planned. As we needed additional income I had temporarily opened a general store in our shop. Our salary from the partnership was used to make the payments on a piece of property we had purchased in Washoe Valley. We had invested our funds into this small ranch so that we would always have a home after the hotel was restored. It also offered us a temporary retreat when business at the hotel became too hectic and we could sit among the pine trees for a brief rest. Our investment was based on the mortgage obligations being met by our partnership salary.

We needed to have a shop opened to keep us in a stable financial position and it was for the purpose of buying stock for this shop that I had gone to Reno. It was on this trip that I was asked to consent to a television show about the Goldfield Hotel.

Several weeks previously Dennis and I had attended a barbecue given by my daughter Lisa. Among her many guests was the co-producer of a national television show with local programming. We were unaware of this fact as we were relating stories of the Goldfield Hotel to other guests at the party and I did not know that the co-producer of the television series was also listening to the conversation.

So I was surprised by this request when I returned to Reno.

Dennis was excited over the news and we agreed it would be great publicity for the hotel as we assumed the program would be based on the reopening of a historical building. I was told to expect a telephone call from the television station within a few days to set up an appointment date for filming.

We had a busy schedule in the hotel but we could set aside a few days while they filmed the program. We had a shop to operate, tours to be given, although they were no longer by donations, a huge building to maintain, and also manage day to day household activities. We also hosted many reporters and interested novice historians as we had done for many years.

Several days later I received the call from the show's co-producer. She had made arrangements for her television crew to be at the hotel within ten days. I told her they would all be welcome and that we would arrange sleeping quarters for them and I would be happy to provide their meals.

I then asked her what the subject matter would be.

She said. "It's the ghost story of the hotel and the title is 'I Live with Ghosts.' In fact we're bringing a paraphsychologist with us, if you don't mind."

I was shocked. "A ghost story? I can't have a ghost story done, it would be like making a joke of the Goldfield Hotel. I don't want the building exploited."

She assured me that the story would be done in good taste, and that if I felt that it wasn't, they wouldn't air any part I felt was offensive. "Besides, Shirley," she said "the schedule has already been made and the crew is planning on being there."

I told her if the story would not embarrass the hotel and if our partner agreed to the subject matter of the program then she could complete her plans for the Goldfield Hotel program.

I contacted our new partner and he felt there was nothing objectionable as far as he was concerned and so our filming date was scheduled as originally planned.

Although our partner had agreed to this program the spirits hadn't and life at the hotel became a private hell. Now they were angry and I sensed their wrath immediately. Now they were coming out to communicate with me because of this anger.

"Why are you doing this to us, why are you holding us up to ridicule. Why, why, why?" That's all I heard every time I entered the right wing to use the bathroom facilities.

In order to wash our clothing I had to use these facilities. I wanted everything neatly washed and pressed upon the arrival of the T.V. crew as we would be too busy at that time to care for any clothing.

I had to bathe, I had to shampoo my hair, I had to wash and brush my teeth. I had to use these facilities many times a day. And each time I heard the same words. "Why are you doing this to us, why are you holding us up to ridicule?"

"No! No!" I would shout in return, "you don't understand, I'm not ridiculing you, they just want to do a story. We're not making fun of you."

I would then run into the safety of the lobby, crying out, "Oh God, I've got to get out of here."

I was torn between several factions, it was like a mental tug-of-war. I loved the old building and wanted to stay and protect it, but then, I wanted to leave bcause I couldn't live with these spirits any longer, and I was now terribly concerned that they may not let me go.

For the first time I worried about their actions. Would they possibly harm the television crew? They were so angry about the filming I didn't know what to expect of them when the crew arrived. I only knew one thing for sure, that after the television filming was over I was going to think seriously about residing in the hotel any longer.

Fire of 1923, Elks Lodge, Tribune Building, and the Goldfield Hotel

Chapter Twenty-Five

Everyone in the town knew that a national television show was coming to Goldfield to film a story about the hotel. This was really nothing new to Goldfield as they used the hotel and the town in at least two movies in recent years. One had been filmed during the past year when Dennis and I played host to the crew and cast of the motion picture. But at least the television crew would bring a little excitement into the town.

We had closed our shop for the day so that we could devote our full attention to our guests. I had invited our good friends Rocky and Marilyn Fry to the hotel so they could meet the crew and watch some of the filming. We had also asked our neighbor if she wished to be there as she was very interested in our ghost situation.

The hotel was ready to host its guests. Sleeping quarters had been arranged and a buffet dinner had been planned for the evening.

It was early in the day when a large van pulled up in front of the hotel bearing the name of the television series. The crew had arrived. There were the co-producer, the host of the television show and the cameraman. They unloaded their equipment including a large television camera which sat on a tripod.

After all introductions were acknowledged Dennis offered to show them through the hotel after they had rested from their long drive from Reno. We talked for awhile about the events in the building but then they decided to look the hotel over as they would be with us for only twenty-four hours and would have to begin filming almost immediately. The co-producer informed me that the parapsychologist would be arriving by late afternoon but they would be filming the building before her arrival.

As Dennis led the crew up the stairway to the second floor the cameraman asked, "Are you sure they won't hurt my camera?" It was not the first time he had posed this question. He seemed greatly concerned about his camera and he had asked me several times before if the ghosts would harm it.

I had assured him that they wouldn't. "They've never done anything like that before," I told him. "You know that they are here and they make sounds but they never do anything physical."

He seemed so upset over leaving his camera that our neighbor graciously offered to watch it for him. She was sitting in an old moroccan leather chair and she placed the camera, which was sitting on the tripod, directly in front of her.

I laughed at the idea of the ghosts harming the camera but if he felt safer with someone sitting with it then at least he could tour through the hotel without any worry.

Our friend Rocky was standing near our neighbor who was watching the camera and Marilyn and I were by the piano talking about this silly situation.

"Marilyn," I said, you've never seen my spooky room, would you like to see it now?"

Marilyn readily accepted my offer and I turned from the piano and started to walk toward the right wing.

I stopped suddenly as I heard a commotion and my neighbor screaming, "It's hostile, it's hostile."

I looked behind me and saw my neighbor trying to hold down the camera which was shaking violently. Her head was thrown backward and she had a look of terror on her face. Each of her feet was pressed against a leg of the tripod as she tried to steady the camera.

I screamed at her as I didn't know what was causing this."what are you doing, what are you doing to the camera?"

I ran over to her and pushed my hands firmly down on top of the camera trying to stop the shaking. My neighbor kept shouting that it was hostile while I was yelling at the camera, "Stop it, stop it."

Even admist all the confusion the thought suddenly occurred to me as to who was responsible for this and I looked upward toward the ceiling and screamed, "Knock it off up there." The camera immediately ceased shaking. It was all over.

Our neighbor showed us her feet. There were indentations on both ankles where she had tried to hold the tripod still by pressing her ankles against its legs. Her hosiery was also torn by this pressure. She was very frightened and upset and excused herself from the hotel saying that she had to get away from this for awhile. I was devastated by this latest occurrence and tried to find an explanation from my friends Marilyn and Rocky. Rocky said at first he thought it was a joke until he saw the look on my neighbor's face and then he realized that she was not controlling the movement of the camera.

I ran up the stairs to find the cameraman. I found him with the others in one of the upper suites. I could barely speak as I was trembling and in a shaky voice inquired, "Is there any reason your camera could start shaking all by itself?" I was actually hoping he had a good answer to my question, but he took one look at me and ran down the hallway to the stairs. We all followed him into the lobby where he quickly retrieved his camera and tripod and put them back into the van. This matter was the point of discussion for awhile but finally the camera was brought back into the hotel and filming of the interior began.

The rest of the afternoon was uneventful and except for the television crew working on their project the hotel was quiet and still.

By early evening the parapsychologist and her husband arrived in Goldfield. I had never met a parapsychologist before and I didn't quite know what to expect. I was then introduced to a lovely and gracious lady who spoke in an eloquent manner and I was delighted to welcome her and her equally amiable husband into our hotel.

We talked briefly as we stood in the lobby but then the television crew informed us that they wanted to film the right wing before it became dark in Goldfield.

The cameraman set up his camera at the entry of the old corridor. Dennis had previously closed all the doors to the rooms in the hallway, so the parapsychologist, upon opening them, could sense anything unusual in each individual room.

I stood next to the cameraman while holding onto my friend Marilyn for emotional support. Dennis and the other crew members stayed in the background as the parapsychologist walked down the corridor by herself.

As she opened the second door on the right side of the hallway she said, "My, my, there are a lot of spirits in here." I was surprised at her remark as we were never sure of the story we had been told about that particular room.

Several years before, an elderly man had come to Goldfield and had walked into Grant Downing's shop and spent several hours talking to Grant about the "old Goldfield." Grant had invited us over to hear one of the old man's tales.

He told us he knew all about the hotel and then told of a high grade assay office that was located in the right wing.

"Yep," he said, "them old high gradin' miners would go to that assay office to sell their gold, but more often than not, they'd take their gold, knock em on their heads and throw them down a trap door."

I had heard many old tales about the hotel during the years we had spent in Goldfield. Some of the stories we found hard to believe and some were very factual. This story interested me because there was a room fitting his description, a large room that had originally been two rooms. A separation wall had been removed but two original doors remained although one of them was locked and the doorknob removed. It was large enough to have housed an office and we were using this room to store books and excess clothing. When I had occasion to enter this room I always felt a low spot as I walked across the tattered rug that partially covered the hardwood floor. When the old man mentioned the trap door I gave more credence to his story as I was sure that a trap door could be the cause of a lowered section of the floor.

I was impressed by his tale as he seemed so certain of the facts.

When I returned to the hotel I asked Dennis to roll back the rug so we could see what was underneath. Close to the center of the floor we found the old trap door. It did not have any hinges, it was just a decaying piece of wood covering an opening in the floor that led down into the basement.

I turned to Dennis. "If someone could go down through that hole, then someone could also come up. Maybe you should nail it up or something."

Dennis cut a piece of plywood that would sufficiently cover the opening and nailed it shut.

I had often wondered if the story the old man had told me was factual. Did they really have a secret high-grading assay office in this room and did they really throw their customers into the basement? High-grading miners couldn't sell their gold to a legitimate assay office as high-grading gold meant stealing it while working in a mine.

When I heard the parapsychologist make that remark about the room I thought that maybe the old man knew exactly what he was talking about.

After she closed the door to the double room she continued on to the far end of the hallway opening each door and looking into every room. She then started back toward us checking each room on the opposite side of the corridor.

She opened the door to room 109, closed it and opened the next door which was the entry to the bathroom. Then she stepped backwards into the hall and reentered 109, closing the door behind her. It seemed as though she was in the room for a long time and in my highly nervous state I turned to the cameraman and said, "She's never coming out of there."

I grabbed Marilyn's arm as I heard the door of room 109 open. As the parapsychologist walked toward the camera she said, "I wouldn't stay in this hotel, not in this wing anyway. A girl died in there, she was chained and couldn't get out." She then looked at me, "My dear lady," she said, "if I were you, I wouldn't take a bath in that bathroom, in fact, I'd take a bath in the hotel in Tonopah."

I just stood there in sheer fright as I listened to her, still holding on to Marilyn's arm.

After that filming we all adjourned to the lobby where the charming parapsychologist sat on one of the black leather settees while the host of the television program conducted an interview with her. I was impressed by the intelligence and knowledge of this woman and I listened intensely to every word she said. She questioned Dennis and I at length about our strange attachment to the hotel and of the events leading up to our purchase of the property.

The interview took over an hour and when it was over I set out the buffet supper that I had prepared in advance.

We all sat in the lobby as we leisurely ate our dinner and discussed the spirits in the hotel. I was conversing with the parapsychologist when she asked, "Shirley, did you ever get vibrations from the elevator cage?"

"No." I answered. "I've never even walked into the elevator on this floor. The cage is actually on the fourth floor and the elevator doors in the lobby were never opened until several months ago when the mechanical engineer pried them open to make an inspection." I explained to her that the elevator had originally descended into the basement, but for some reason the shaft was boarded up at the lobby level many years ago. What appeared to be the floor of the elevator cage was actually now the bottom of the shaft.

I repeated to her that the lobby floor elevator doors had been locked long before we purchased the hotel and even though the mechanical engineer left them open for a later inspection, I had never walked into the shaft.

"Do you get vibrations from the elevator shaft?" I asked.

"Oh yes," she replied, "very strong vibrations."

I couldn't understand why she was getting vibrations in the elevator shaft. What did the elevator have to do with the spirits in the right wing or Mr. G. in the dining room? I sat quietly for awhile while I mentally explored all the possibilities.

And then it finally occurred to me.

I asked her, "Can you get vibrations in the elevator shaft

from something on another floor, something close to the elevator?"

"Of course," she answered.

I became very excited. It had to be the bones, the bones Lisa had found when she was digging under the basement walkway which was directly next to the elevator shaft. What had been buried there and what had taken place in that section of the basement that had caused this sensitive lady to receive such strong vibrations? I shuddered at the thought of what might have happened in the basement during the long forgotten past.

I told the parapsychologist the details of the day that Lisa and I were digging by the stairway and Lisa had dug under the walkway only to find bones.

As I was relating this story to her I came to the realization that somehow I had to leave this hotel. I was beginning to feel enveloped by these spirits and since the arrival of the television crew it seemed that they were determined to brazenly make their presences known.

It was now late in the evening and as we had been talking for hours everyone agreed when the suggestion was made that it was time to get some sleep.

The parapsychologist and her husband were the first ones to leave as they had a thirty minute drive ahead of them to reach their hotel room in Tonopah. Even as I wished them goodnight I was looking forward to their early morning return as I had enjoyed their company immensely. We then sat and talked with Marilyn and Rocky discussing the day's events and in particular the camera episode. I was thankful that Rocky had witnessed the incident as he was a stable and intelligent local businessman and very well know in Goldfield. He would not jeopardize his good reputation by substantiating this occurrence if it were not true. She told us repeatedly that at first he believed that the neighbor was just playing and shaking the camera intentionally. He than saw the look of fear on her face and noticed her ankles positioned tightly against the tripod legs and with her hands clamped strongly on top of the camera he realized it was impossible for her to be controlling it.

Shortly afterwards Marilyn and Rocky said they were tired and decided to go home.

After our guests had departed I asked the television crew where they preferred to sleep as they would be staying overnight. I had prepared the upstairs bedrooms for them but they said that they would feel much more comfortable in the dining room.

I could understand why they choose the safety of the dining room as compared to sleeping on the upper floor. I had made the same decision many times before as the dining room offered an easy access to the street. I could also sympathize with their apprehensions about the hotel as it had been an unexpectedly frightening day. I lived in this atmosphere for years but these people were strangers to the building and it must have been quite upsetting to them.

Dennis and I would now be using the upstairs bedroom as our beds in the dining room would be used by the television crew.

The electric lights in the hallway leading to the bedrooms had been turned off earlier in the day by shutting off the main breaker switch. I had Dennis cut off the power when I noticed a light arcing when I flicked on a light switch in the hallway. It was very minor but as I had a tendency to worry over the electrical system I thought it would be safer to shut off all power on that floor until the receptacle could be checked.

I had never been afraid to walk throughout this floor in the dark but that particular night I felt an uneasiness about going upstairs and not having any light. Dennis turned off the lamps in the lobby and said it was time that we both get some rest. I hesitated for a moment and gave the lobby a long lingering look. How beautiful it was and how much a part of me it had become.

By flashlight I led the way up the darkened stairway into our room. I undressed quickly, crawled into the old iron bed and slid under the warmth of the blankets. I was very tired and I needed the rest as filming would begin again early the next morning.

But sleep was not to come. Not yet. I stiffened as I sensed

their presence in the quiet of the night. What did they want with me now?

"Why did you do this to us, why do you hold us up to ridicule?"

"No! Not again. Go away, for God's sake leave me alone and let me sleep. I called out to Dennis, I wanted to go downstairs, but I was afraid, there were no lights, I couldn't make it downstairs.

"Dennis, please, I want to sleep in the van. Get up, take me downstairs, please!"

Dennis responded with a definite "No"!

What was I going to do now? I couldn't stay in this room but I was too frightened to get up from my bed and venture out into the hallway alone.

"Dennis, please! I can't sleep here."

His answer was the same.

As I laid there, shaking uncontrollably with fear, I made up my mind to leave the hotel and move to my home in the valley near Reno. Five years of living with ghosts had taken its toll. I would leave and never come back.

"Don't leave , Shirley." Again they were reading my thoughts.

"Don't leave? If you don't want me to leave, why do you do this to me? Why don't you let me sleep?"

Then, almost apologetically, "We're sorry, Shirley."

"Sorry? If you're sorry, go away, please just go away. I'm leaving here, I'm never coming back."

And then . . . the words that penetrated deep into my soul, words that will haunt me forever. "But you can't leave, Shirley."

"What do you mean, I can't leave?"

"You can't leave Shirley, you're one of us."

"What do you mean I'm one of you? For God's sake, what are you telling me? What do you want of me?"

I couldn't believe this was happening. If I was one of them, that meant I had to have lived here before. Was it possible? Was this the reason I was drawn to this old mining town, why I gave up everything to fight for the hotel? Is this why I would sit on the porch steps and curse this town because Goldfield as it used to be, was gone? Was I part of its past? Somewhere in another life did I have something to do with the girl in the room? What was I to her? A sister, a friend? Was I her mother? On these thoughts I had no reaction, until . . .

Oh dear God, was I that girl in the room?

With that thought a sense of calmness came over me. At last I understood what they had been trying to tell me for years and realized how long they had been waiting for my return.

I closed my eyes and drifted off to sleep.

Original Goldfield Hotel which burned down on November 17, 1906. left: Boxer Battling Nelson, Helen Douglas Langford, and an unidentified bartender

Chapter Twenty-Six

The sun rose early in the morning and although I was awake at this hour, I was surprised as I went downstairs to see that the television crew was already dressed and sipping coffee in the lobby.

"Good morning Shirley, did you sleep well?" one of the crew asked.

"Pretty well," I answered. "Were you able to sleep in the dining room?"

By their answer I assumed they hadn't slept at all. I was told that at 4:00 a.m. they all got into their van and drove around town until daylight. I also assumed that they felt an old hotel inhabited by ghosts was not conducive to sleeping.

I hurried into the cold corridor as I was anxious to take my bath and dress. I was concerned that the parapsychologist would arrive early and I desperately needed to speak to her. I had to tell her what had happened the night before.

I was extremely nervous and found it hard to concentrate on anything except what the spirits had told me. Could it possibly be true?

I paced the floors for two hours before I saw her car being parked in front of the hotel. I rushed up to her as she entered the lobby and pleaded to her, "Please, please, tell me, do I have a vivid imagination, am I losing my mind or can spirits really communicate with me?" I then told her about the messages I received from these entities.

"No, my dear, you are not losing your mind. Mental telepathy is greater than most people believe it is. You died in that room, Shirley, you were that girl in the room. I knew it last night but I didn't want to upset you. My husband and I talked about it on the way to Tonopah. But you were wrong about one thing. You said you felt the girl was about sixteen. I think she was closer to nineteen. And you looked the same in that life as you did in this one. That's why you saw a tall, slender girl with dishwater blonde hair."

"But then, why am I so afraid of her?" I asked. "Why am I so terrified of the room?"

"Because of the memory," she answered. "It's your memory that's recalling the terror."

At that moment I felt compelled to go into the room. "Please excuse me," I said and I quickly walked toward the entry of the right wing.

I heard the co-producer's voice call out to me as I passed by the registry desk, "Shirley, don't go in there, you'll get upset and we have to start filming very soon." I kept walking. I had to go into 109 and without hesitation I boldly flung open the door and stepped into the room.

"You're not here any longer," I shouted, "you're gone, I'm here! Do you understand, you're gone." I knew I sounded like a mad woman shrieking these words into a vacant room but I couldn't stop.

"Was this really my room, Oh dear God, was this really my room?" I then stood silently in the center of the room staring at the walls and trying to remember. As I gazed at the wall by the doorway I felt a very strange sensation and then I saw it. It was my dresser, just for an instant I saw my dresser.

"Oh, my God", I yelled, "it's my dresser." But in that fleeting moment I had seen something else too. Near the top of the large dresser mirror but to the right were two small holes in the wall. Now, as I looked at the wall, I could only see wallpaper. I knew I had seen those holes when I saw the dresser. If I could find them, then I would know I had actually been in this room years ago. I was almost hysterical at this time but I had to find out, I had to know the truth.

I looked closely at the wallpaper, searching for any sign of the paper being pasted over the holes. I was looking for anything, a slight indentation, a spot not firmly adhered to the wall, a bubble under the wallpaper, just anything that looked out of the ordinary.

All I saw were small pinholes which would have been

made when air bubbles were under the paper and the usual way to get them out was to puncture them with a straight pin.

I made up my mind that I was not going to leave this room until I found out if the holes were actually in the wall. I then started tearing the wallpaper away in large sheets. Some of the smaller pieces clung to the wall and I scraped furiously to get them off.

As I tore the paper from the wall I found myself shouting again. "Who put this wallpaper on my wall, this isn't my paper." It was my voice but I did not understand why I was saying it.

I couldn't find the holes and I was about to give up my search when I pulled away one last piece that was further to the right. I almost slumped to the floor when I saw the holes. I looked over to the old iron twin bed that we had set up in this room and said aloud, "And my bed was here, right where this one is, my bed was here."

I then opened the door of the closet that terrified me and feeling a pang of revulsion I knew something terrible had happened in there.

I ran into the lobby and found the cameraman there. "Jim, Jim, come here, I have to show you something." As we walked back toward room 109 I tried to tell him what had occurred. As I told him, I kept saying, "It's true, I'm not making it up, I really saw the holes, I really saw the dresser."

Jim said, "Lady, I'd believe anything you told me about this hotel, especially after staying here."

I pointed out the holes to him as we stood on the wallpaper that littered the floor. He went back into the lobby and got his camera and asked me to tear off more wallpaper while he filmed me doing it.

When he was through filming I walked into the dining room. I already knew the answer but I had to ask the question anyway. I had wondered so often why Mr. G. came to me in time of trouble. Tommy had said that the old Irishman told him the girl was locked in the room by her father because she had become pregnant by a married man and who had a better opportunity to meet this girl than the man who frequented the hotel so often

I stood under the ceiling where my friendly spirit walked and said, "Mr. G., what was I to you?" His answer, "you were my sweetheart, you were my Sal."

I then asked, "Why did you let them do this to me?" And then almost softly, "I didn't know, I really didn't know."

I then left the dining room and went upstairs to find the parapsychologist. She was with Dennis who was giving her an extended tour of the upper floors. I explained to her briefly about seeing my dresser and finding the holes, but not wishing to interrupt her tour, I returned to the lobby.

I was finding it very difficult to accept this. These things happened to other people, not to me. This was something you would read about in a magazine, not something that pertained to one's own life. I felt dazed as if the world around me was unreal. I would walk from room to room, then sit in the lobby, then get up and walk again. My thoughts ran from the practical to the bizarre.

One of my first thoughts was to have Dennis move my furniture and clothing into Room 109 and go back to where I belonged. I knew I had to discard that idea as I could see what the results would be. How long would it be before I became so attached to the past that I would lose my touch with reality?

Then my thoughts turned back to the events in my childhood. Why was I so deathly afraid of closets? Did it have something to do with the closet in 109? What about the coyotes I would envision on a moonlit night when I was a little girl in Chicago, or the driving urge I felt to go west and live in the desert? Did it start way back then? Was I meant to eventually find Goldfield and come home? I thought about our long struggle to keep the hotel, our fierce determination to protect the building no matter what we had to suffer.

I remember the dreams I had for years before we purchased the Goldfield Hotel. They would always be the same. I would be running through a house, opening doors and finding more rooms and then opening another door only to find more rooms behind it, and the rooms were always endless.

And how did I match the brown paint in the saloon so perfectly, the day I insisted it had to be a certain shade?

And what about the anger I felt when I looked out the window at the ruins of Goldfield, the bitter resentment I felt about the original building being gone?

Was it because I had lived in Goldfield in the past? Everything seemed to support this theory but my mind rebelled against it and I wanted to scream. "No, it isn't true."

If it was true, why was I drawn back here? Was there a mystery I had to solve? Was the girl murdered, was I supposed to uncover these facts, and what was I supposed to do now that I knew?

I was relieved when the sound of voices interrupted my thoughts. Dennis was coming down the stairs with the parapsychologist and the members of the television crew There was to be one more interview with the parapsychologist before she left Goldfield, but before the interview we all went into room 109 where she sat on the edge of the iron bed and discussed the situation.

I told her I was no longer afraid of the room and she spoke of understanding, that now that I understood, I could accept the spirits being here.

At her last interview she commented that she knew Dennis had also been at the hotel in a past life but she did not know in what capacity. This is why he also had such a strange attachment to the building and gave up everything we had to protect it.

After this last interview she and her husband left Goldfield for Reno. I was sorry to see them leave but I was grateful that I was given the opportunity to meet such very nice people.

The camera was once again set up in the lobby for the last filming to be done in the hotel. Dennis and I stood behind the registry desk to be interviewed. We had, however, neglected to lock the front door and this oversight caused an incident very similar to the one I had in the old corridor when I was with the three miners from Tonopah.

Everything had to be very quiet for the filming. The host of the television show had just asked me, "Shirley, do the spirits want us here?"

Registry desk where the television crew dropped to the floor.

I started to answer him. "No, they don't, in fact, they're quite upset . . ."

I never finished the sentence as the front door burst open, shattering the silence of the lobby. It was a local resident, saying as he walked in, "Hey, I didn't know you guys were into ghosts, let me tell you what happened when I was up here on your roof."

I was startled by this incident but not as startled as I was to see that two of the crew members had dropped to the floor. I don't know if they appreciated their stay in the hotel, but when the program aired, one of the last comments the television host said at the end of his show was, "I never believed in ghosts until I stayed at the Goldfield Hotel."

This incident did help ease the tension I felt and although I felt sympathetic towards the television crew, I found it difficult to do the interview while trying to hold back my laughter.

By late afternoon the crew had loaded their equipment into their van and were on their way back to Reno. I had enjoyed their company and sincerely wished they could have stayed longer but I personally felt that they were anxious to leave.

As their van pulled away I realized that it was just Dennis and I in the hotel again and although I was not afraid of the room any longer the thought of being alone with the ghosts seemed like more than I could bear.

They had been very quiet since they had told me that I was "one of them" It was as if they were embarrassed by their actions when the television crew was here and were quietly standing by to see my reaction to having been the girl in the room.

I had always sensed that there were entities hovering in the corridor. At least two seemed to be young girls. Many times I would get a strange feeling that they were peering at me from behind the bathroom door and giggling, as sisters might.

I also felt the presence of other entities. One seemed to be female, older and quiet, the other a male who seemed to stay in the background just watching. I thought of the numerous times I felt these presences when I was in the bathroom next to 109, especially when I was using the mirror. I sensed them strongly and knew they were watching my every move as if they were interested in everything I was doing. If I hadn't been so frightened of them. I possibly would have realized that they were just concerned and wanted to be near me.

I also thought back to the night over five years ago when our neighbors from California visited us and told us how they sensed many eyes staring at them and felt their coldness. Our neighbors were not frightened, just aware of them. Looking back I can understand that they were just curious and had to look our friends over.

One fact I was always aware of during all the years in the hotel was that these spirits would not harm me nor would they harm our friends or anyone with good intentions towards us. I had never felt that I was in any danger from these entities.

After reliving many incidents in my mind, I finally found an explanation for the unusual way I would greet the hotel after being on a prolonged absence. I would open the front door and step into the lobby shouting, "I'm back, I'm home." I would feel very foolish at times saying this but I felt compelled to do so and I always thought I was speaking to the hotel. But was I? Did I somehow know, even then, that I was really coming home?

It was now later in the afternoon and I decided to find my friend Don, a resident of Goldfield. I wanted him to know what had happened in 109. I did not want these personal events to be common knowledge, in fact, I had suggested that none of this be mentioned on the upcoming program that was due to appear on television very soon.

I didn't have to look very far for Don as he just happened to be walking past the side entrance of the building. I called to him to come inside and as we walked toward 109 I started relating the story to him. I was surprised to find that Don was very interested in spirits and cited an experience of his own.

I was able to be in this room now without fear and I took advantage of this by looking the room over throughly.

"Don, look, look at this bathroom door. It's all nailed up."

Don walked over to where I was standing in front of the bathroom door and ran his fingers over the nails. They had been nailed into the doorframe and then bent into the door and hammered down. There had to be at least fifty nails securing this door.

"Don," I said, "why would someone go through the trouble of nailing this door shut unless they wanted to make sure it couldn't be opened?"

This door led into the bathroom from room 109 but the bathroom also had another door opening into the corridor so it could be used by other guests. On each side of the bathroom door that led into 109 was a separate lock that could be opened by a skeleton key. This was done for protection. If someone was using the bathroom and had entered through the hallway entrance, they could lock the door from the bathroom side. Any inhabitants of room 109 could lock their side of the door insuring that no one had access to their room through the bathroom. There was no need to nail a door shut under normal conditions and Don had to agree with me.

I was telling him what the parapsychologist had said, that a girl was chained in the room and that it explained why the girl was standing by the center of the wall the day I saw her when the church group insisted that we all stand in a circle and concentrate.

It had always puzzled me that she was not standing by the window. I remember vividly how she looked, her face to the wall and her arms reaching upward as if she were trying to get out. But why wouldn't she try to get through the window? If she were chained she couldn't reach it. This was also the window that had the concrete chute-like abutment that led into the room behind the registry desk.

My mind wandered back to the day I first saw the girl and I was suddenly struck by a terrifying thought. The parapsychologist had said I looked the same in that life as I did in my present one. What if she had been facing me instead of the wall, or what if she had turned around? Would I have seen the face of my childhood upon that girl? And if I had? . . . I shuddered at the very thought.

I was so engrossed in these thoughts that I barely heard Don speaking to me. "See, Shirley, here's the chain marks."

Don was kneeling on the floor next to a short steam pipe that held the radiator valve. The radiator had been moved but this connection was still there.

Don continued, "I can feel them with my hands, something was chained and was scraping against it."

"Are you sure, Don?" I asked. "Couldn't they possibly have been made by a wrench if someone was trying to tighten it or something?"

He answered, "There's nothing here to tighten, there's no connection. Just a piece of pipe with the valve on it."

I was trying to find a logical explanation for everything and I did not want to purposely build up evidence proving that a girl was actually held in this room. I just wanted the truth. But the evidence was appearing to be here. I found myself staring at the opening of the crawl space in this room, the same opening that was in each of the right wing rooms, the opening that enabled maintenance men to enter the basement below for repairs. The small door to this opening in 109 was standing against the wall. Something was bothering me about this door and I strained my memory trying to remember what it was.

And then I remembered. Months before when the mechanical engineer was inspecting the water and radiator systems he had an occasion to use these openings. During that time he had asked Dennis to borrow a claw hammer as the door to this opening had been nailed shut.

I then pointed out to Don the holes in the wall and went into more detail about how I found them and the story behind it. Don examined them very closely. He said, "Shirley, these look like they were made by the bottom of the legs of a chair or maybe a small table. Usually they have those little caps on the bottom of the legs and if someone banged the chair against the wall, it would make this kind of hole."

I started to laugh and said, "Don the parapsychologist said I looked the same in my previous life and inferred that I was the same type of person that I am now. If that's true and someone did lock me up in this room, I damn well would have bashed a chair or something against a wall, and that's probably why I was chained."

When Don and I ended our investigation of the room we were left with these facts A bathroom door heavily secured by being nailed shut, an opening into the basement that had also been nailed, scrapes on a pipe just inches away from where I had seen the girl, scrapes that very possibly were made by a chain. And there was the window to consider. This was the only room in the entire hotel that had a window that did not open to the outdoors.

Although these facts could not prove positively that a girl was held captive in this room, it did suggest very strongly that someone had gone to a lot of trouble to secure room 109.

Recalling a 1918 inventory of the hotel that we had received from the historical society, I remember that it showed beyond a doubt that room 109 was used for storage. Why would this room, a room larger than most and the only one in the right wing with an adjoining bath and oversize

closet, be chosen for a storage room? Was someone ad-
versed to using109 again for anything but storage, and if so,
what secrets were they trying to lock away along with
discarded furnishings?

After Don left the hotel I walked onto the front porch and
sat on one of the old benches. The last two days had been
very exhausting, both mentally and emotionally and I had
to have a time of quiet. Twilight had already descended
over Goldfield and I could be assured I would not be interrupted as it was very seldom that anyone stopped by the
hotel at this hour. Here I could sit in solitude and enjoy the
cool October breezes.

The time I had spent with Don investigating the room
had put me in a relaxed frame of mind and helped me to
accept the truth about the spirits. Talking about the situation with this understanding friend almost normalized the
events of the past days.

I was anxious to go on a quest for the truth. I did not
expect that any of this would be a matter of record so I
would have to search elsewhere for the answers to the
many questions that plaqued me.

My search, however would have to be delayed temporarily as I had more pressing business to attend to. Cold
weather would be coming to Goldfield in a few short weeks
and improvements on a heating system had not been made
as promised, nor had the plumbing been installed for our
planned delicatessen.

I was becoming concerned about these agreements that
had not been honored as we would not only need the heat
for the winter months but we would need the income from
our delicatessen.

I was also concerned when I saw some of the plans for the
hotel's restoration. Walls were to be torn down, modern
bathrooms were to replace the turn of the century facilities,
and extensive gaming was to abound in the beautiful old
lobby. I was totally against these plans and it was definitely
not in keeping with the1907 theme that we had agreed upon
and I was devastated when I heard they may possibly tear
out the entire right wing for a slot machine area. I did not

want the Goldfield Hotel turned into a Las Vegas or Reno type casino hotel.

And what would the spirits think of all this, or worse, what would they do about it?

Not wishing to ruin my evening on the porch worrying about these problems, I temporarily put them out of my mind. I was also at ease now with the spirits and I could live in the hotel without apprehensions. Where their presence previously had surrounded me with fear, I now felt surrounded by their love and protection.

It was dark now in Goldfield and I could see the twinkle of the lights from the homes that dotted the desert streets with the faint outline of the Malapai mountains behind them. How beautiful it was. I wondered how I could have ever considered leaving this town that I had grown to love, this town that had become so much a part of me.

The scene from the porch was an all too familiar one. The occasional car driving down the lonely highway, the tinkling of the piano from the nearby saloon, the old mining shacks, and the ruins of early Goldfield silhouetted against the horizon. It was exactly the same, the same as it was the first evening I sat on this old front porch. I knew then I could never leave this town or my beloved Goldfield Hotel.

I heard Dennis as he walked onto the front porch and quietly asked, "Don't you want to come back into the hotel now?"

I looked up at him. "Yes, Dennis, I do."

Fire Station No. 1, Esmeralda County Courthouse, Hose Company

Epilogue

Four weeks after the filming of the national television show, it was all over.

We were informed by our partnership that we were no longer needed as agents of the hotel and we were to vacate the premises. The keys to the building would be turned over to the neighbor who had agreed to "look after the hotel", the same neighbor that was involved in the camera incident who said the spirits were hostile. Although I was devastated by the news I was not totally shocked by it. Before we had signed the partnership agreement I had serious misgivings and had told Dennis repeatedly that "we would never be a part of the hotel operation and we wouldn't see any money for at least ten years", My intuition had not proven me wrong and I was disillusioned and bitter.

Gone were our plans of residing in the hotel until the restoration was completed as we had been promised. Gone were our hopes of opening our delicatessen in the shop our partner had promised to bring up to specifications. But most of all I knew then that the assurances made to Dennis and I that we would always be a part of the hotel were shattered.

We also had invested the initial funds we received from the partnership into a small property in Washoe Valley south of Reno, relying on our hotel salary to meet our monthly obligation. Once again we had placed our trust and faith in someone only to find ourselves in yet another struggle.

Dennis and I wanted to leave immediately for Washoe Valley to begin manufacturing our product in time for the Christmas season but we foolishly agreed to stay in the hotel without salary to oversee roof repairs that were to begin in a few days. As usual due to many delays nothing materialized on the roofing project until almost two months later and we finally left Goldfield a week before Christmas. too late for our holiday business and too late for our property. It was December, 1981.

The years that followed were extremely difficult both financially and physically. Dennis and I had tried many ways to earn a living but it was not easy to do so because it came to a point where the only place we called home was our van. Once out of sheer desperation I contacted our partner offering to sell him a small percentage of our interest in the hotel if we could start up our business again and get on with our lives. His answer was "No".

During this period of time the locks were changed on the hotel doors and we were denied access to the building except by expressed permission. I was very concerned about all of our possessions we had left in the hotel because of the many functions being held in the building, and so I contacted our partner requesting entry and telling him of my concern. I was told that I would need the permission of the neighbor who was in charge of the keys and she would unlock the door and allow me to enter the building. As we still owned a percentage of the property I felt it was degrading to beg entry from someone not financially involved in the hotel so I declined his offer. At a later date we did have occasion to enter the hotel and found that many of our possessions were no longer there.

Also during this time I frequently attempted to contact my partner requesting the status of the restoration and other business pertinent to the hotel. On the rare occasions that I was allowed to speak to him I was told that as a limited partner we had no voice in any of the transactions and furthermore, it was "none of our business". I would recall his words at times like this, the words he uttered before we signed the agreement, "Shirley, I need your experience and expertise and I cannot go ahead with this project without you and Dennis". Obviously he could.

The only report that I received on the hotel came from the news on television about the upcoming reopening of the hotel and from friends in Goldfield. I heard about the auctions, filming and the numerous tours being given of

the building. It also came to my attention that Room 109 was
shown as the ghost room and the girl in the room was called
"Gertie the ghost". Using a small portion of my story of the
actual events occuring in Room 109, a completely and totally untrue version of the girl was being related to tourists
and to at least one news reporter. A stain on the wall in this
room which I knew to be nothing more than a huge water
mark was being pawned off as the ghostly image of a girl.
I was enraged over this and told Dennis, "they have taken
everything away from us, now they are even taking my
story"

We were also assured at the onset of our new partnership
that the restoration would be completed in a year but at this
writing almost four years later the hotel stands as it did the
day we put our signatures on the Limited Partnership
Agreements with the exception of a few repairs.

Our frustrations at being the outcasts of a partnership are
nearing an end as our lives have stabilized and although we
live on a moderate income we are looking forward to finally
bringing litigation against our partner.

At these times I look out my living room window that
frames the foothills in Reno. But I know that beyond those
hills lies the twisting desert road that leads to Goldfield and
I wonder, "Will I ever see my beautiful Goldfield Hotel
again? Will I ever be able to go home?"

It is November, 1985.

To My Readers

It is January 1991 and time to take my manuscript off the shelf, shake off the dust and send it off to press.

For the past five years Dennis and I have been living quite comfortably in Reno surrounded by family and my grandchildren. In 1986 we had accepted a moderate settlement from the partnership after we were finally able to retain an attorney to represent us in a lawsuit against our partner. However our long struggle had taken its toll both physically and financially and we found we could not afford to pursue the litigation in the manner that we wanted to so we reluctantly agreed to a settlement.

With the proceeds from the settlement we were able to place a down payment on a house, receive medical attention and provide a good home for our dogs Dini and Bruno. Gabriel had been lost to us years before. Dini left us a year ago dying unexpectedly when she was fifteen and Bruno suffering the loss of his constant companion passed away shortly afterwards at the age of twenty-two. With tear streaked eyes Dennis painfully built their little caskets and we quietly buried them in the pet cemetery in Carson City. The loss of our faithful dogs left an emptiness in our lives that can never be filled and it seemed to close another door on our Goldfield days. They were so much a part of our lives in the hotel and stood by loyally even under the most adverse conditions and I still find it hard to believe that they are gone.

As far as the hotel is concerned it is up for sale having been placed into receivership due to the partnership's bankruptcy. On a fairly recent trip to Goldfield I was able to view what I refer to as the destruction of the Goldfield Hotel. As I stood outside of the building my worst fears were realized. Walls had been torn down, original doors, window sills and woodwork were replaced, sections of the old corridor and all the rooms including 109 had been gutted and a hideous silo type structure loomed in the backyard. This is what was meant when I insisted he keep the hotel as original as possible, when my partner agreed to "use his best efforts to do so", the building was well on its way to becoming a Las Vegas-Reno style hotel casino. The original historical Goldfield Hotel was gone and future tourists will be denied the pleasure of seeing the building as it was in 1907. A major part of Nevada's history was lost.

For the second time in my life I looked up at this huge structure and cried out, "What have they done to you and who had the right to do this?" I recalled the day I warned my former partner about his plans to destroy the right wing. It was shortly before the filming of the television show and he announced that he was going to tear out the right wing for additional slot machine area.

I was greatly upset over the latest development but I also knew what would happen if he removed the right wing. I told him, "Don't do this, don't disturb it, if you do you will have nothing but problems." But he did.

As I strolled through Goldfield it was if I were walking through a ghost town. It was not like the Goldfield I knew. So many of the older residents had passed on or moved away. Everything had changed and most of the old businesses were either vacant or modernized.

As I looked across the street from the hotel I thought of our dear friends Helen and Grant Downing, of the shop they had there and all of the enjoyable times we had spent together. It was always Dennis and Grant and Helen and I. We lost Grant several years before and it is difficult to accept that our dear friend is gone. Helen is alone now and living in Deming, New Mexico where she has the companionship of her daughter Lureen. She will celebrate her eightieth birthday this year and is in the process of opening a new shop. Helen and I frequently speak of Goldfield and of the days we shared together but we both agree that it is over, an end of an era and a closed chapter of our lives. Goldfield and the hotel is no longer what it used to be and I must relinquish these memories to the past.

In re-reading this manuscript that I had written many years ago I found myself questioning all of the transactions that occured during the time Dennis and I owned the hotel, transactions that would place us in a more serious position than we had been in before. In most cases we did not have a choice. When we first purchased the hotel we did so with honesty and sincerety and I believed that all of the other parties involved approached us in the same manner. This did not prove to be true but by this time we were not in a financial position to legally handle our business affairs and had to rely in our trust in others. So many times I was in a state of utter frustration as I was well aware of the improper business behavior of the other parties involved. But we did not have any funds available to do anything about it and our first concern was retaining our property, not only because we had invested all of our money into the building but for the strange hold the hotel had on Dennis and I, the feeling that we had to protect the hotel at any cost.

But it is all over now and we have accepted the fact that the hotel as we knew it is gone and we have to be content with memories. For never again will we sit on the old front porch listening for an occasional car traveling down the highway after dark, or the howl of the coyotes interrupting the stillness of the desert. And never again will we be able to watch the lightening storms over Lone Mountain, or listen to Dennis bringing music back into the hotel while playing the piano for the tourists.

The old piano from the lobby now graces our living room and on rare occasions Dennis will play "Oh dem Golden Slippers" and I find myself standing in the old lobby singing for the tourists. It is as if I'm actually there and it is then that I can still feel their presence. I know they are still there waiting for me to come home. Several times during the past few years I have stood silently in front of the old building staring at what used to be the old corridor and can still hear them. "Come back Shirley, there is a way to come back. Come home".

But I can't . . . and still?

Shirley Porter Dybicz